# JOB
# SHARING

## A
## NEW PATTERN FOR QUALITY
## OF
## WORK AND LIFE

by

**GRETL S. MEIER**

February 1979

THE W. E. UPJOHN INSTITUTE FOR EMPLOYMENT RESEARCH

THE INSTITUTE, a nonprofit research organization, was established on July 1, 1945. It is an activity of the W. E. Upjohn Unemployment Trustee Corporation, which was formed in 1932 to administer a fund set aside by the late Dr. W. E. Upjohn for the purpose of carrying on "research into the causes and effects of unemployment and measures for the alleviation of unemployment."

This study is for sale by the Institute at $4.50 per copy. For quantity orders of this publication or any combination of Institute publications, price reductions are as follows: 10-25 copies, 10 percent; 26-50, 15; 51-100, 20; over 100, 25.

To Jerry, Jeremy, Andrew, Daniel, and David—true sharers all.

# THE AUTHOR

Gretl S. Meier is a graduate of Mount Holyoke College (B.A., Political Science), Radcliffe College of Harvard University (M.A., American History), and did further graduate work in International Relations at L'Institut d'Etudes Politiques of the University of Paris. She has been co-director of New Ways to Work, a San Francisco-Palo Alto employment resource agency since 1973 and has served on its Job Sharing Program staff since its inception in 1975. She also has been research assistant at The Brookings Institution, a staff member of the first Mayor's Commission on Puerto Rican Affairs in New York City, and a consultant to the Human Relations Office of the New Haven Unified School District in Union City, California.

Ms. Meier is the author of *Job Sharing in the Schools,* a preliminary study of selected California districts, as well as numerous general articles on job sharing. She co-authored the final report of the CETA sponsored Job Sharing Project of New Ways to Work, and testified in 1976 before the U.S. Senate Subcommittee on Employment, Poverty, and Migratory Labor on the need for alternative work patterns. She has also been concerned with European experiences with work flexibility and their relevance to alternative work patterns in the U.S. In 1978, under a grant from the German Marshall Fund, she represented New Ways to Work at meetings with European colleagues to explore these issues.

When two do the same thing,
it is not the same thing after all.

— Syrus Pubilius
(Roman author, ca. 42 B.C.)

# PREFACE

This study seeks to explore why people want to share jobs, how they have fashioned different arrangements and, above all, what the outcomes are personally—the joys and the stresses. Job sharers are two individuals who hold one position. Job sharing, a new concept in work time, may also provide, in practice, a new work method. We have wanted to examine the experience gained in order to indicate the criteria for success. But because our primary interest lies in the way work affects human beings, the interpretation of "success" necessarily depends on an understanding of this value.

In modern industrial society work has come to mean paid employment in an eight-hour, five-day week job. Its object for the individual is to provide not only economic well being, but also a sense of esteem and an identification of one's place in society. Job sharers are no different, but they have deliberately chosen to gain the ends of work by new means. Although an infinitesimal proportion of all job holders, such individuals, hundreds or thousands at the most, are beginning to test one alternative to the norm. Their efforts to better balance the quality of their own lives may create models for others who feel able, economically and socially, to venture new choices.

Because we believe that what really counts in this subject is not countable, this study will disappoint those who are looking for precise formulae. Nor will it offer a "how to" guide to determine whether job sharing is cost effective for organizations. Instead we hope that, although it will show the complications of change, it will also indicate the potential advantages to employers. These are rarely easy to measure. For this reason, the study will raise more questions than it answers. Furthermore, no amount of statistical data on productivity and labor unit costs would be definitive in providing a rationale for work change—even if such were available. Current practice of job sharing lends itself, instead, to an interpretive survey of the variety of individual cases.

Although the last decade has witnessed growing attention to many forms of work flexibility, the implementation of change moves slowly. Impetus comes primarily from individuals who want more control over their time, as well as a determination in the kinds of work they do. At the same time, agencies concerned with employment policies and the generally elusive "quality of work life" issues are raising public awareness. Management, particularly in the public and service sectors, either attracted by the lure of "two for the price of one" or responsive to changing employee needs, has become curious about the potential of job sharing. Although organized labor has evinced little inclination to initiate alternative work patterns, it has been more willing to accept flextime than part time options.

In the meantime, government has become a prime, if slow, mover by enacting or proposing legislation to permit job sharing by state and federal employees. These efforts, together with those in local government and others in some professions, give credence to the possibility of developing systematic implementation procedures. Few initiatives are in effect as yet.

Since the concept is new and the practice sporadic, the basic vocabulary of job sharing still has to be established. Analysis is difficult if not impossible on the basis of published information. Such literature as exists appears in press and magazine accounts of single teams. Reports of the few experiments in progress offer only tentative findings. In sum, the picture of job sharing is kaleidoscopic. Some jobs have finished; others are just beginning (including more recent examples in the private sector), but almost none have been evaluated in any systematic fashion.

When we look for the background on these current arrangements we realize little is known about the beginnings of job sharing. For the past five years, New Ways to Work has been receiving letters from individuals and teams across the U.S.

describing their experiences. Each partnership feels theirs is a unique situation.

In order to give a more telescopic view, chapter one of this study outlines the evolution of definition and practice in the larger and smaller experiments of the last few years, and suggests the trends which underlie progress in the last decade. It reviews various ways organizations have restructured full time positions for both part time and shared jobs. The description of state and local experiences, particularly, relies on information gathered from interviews with project directors, as well as from their official reports.

Chapters two and three draw on information from our survey in 1977 based on a lengthy questionnaire to several hundred sharers. These sections examine whether the new arrangement is, in practice, *a new way of working per se* as well as a new way to establish part time jobs.

Chapter four offers selected interviews with partners, their supervisors, and some of their full time co-workers. Their comments are more telling than the survey percentages. These team profiles resulted from hundreds of hours of conversations, usually taped, and edited in the interest of brevity and clarity. Most participants, both in questionnaires and in interviews, wanted to talk, some with the self-conscious pride of pioneers, others with a more matter-of-fact acceptance of their job sharing arrangements. In almost all instances, people were eager to articulate their feelings. They care about their work and their jobs.

Chapter five examines policy implications and needs for the future.

The value of this study will lie, we hope, in its capacity to stimulate thought and discussion about an innovative way of working. Social and economic changes of the 1980s will accelerate the challenges to traditional work structure. As policy makers examine measures to increase employment, they will also need to consider flexible work patterns which will meet emerging labor needs and take advantage of education and professional training. This study focuses on job sharing as one means of providing an opportunity for individual choice in the totality of daily and life patterns.

## ACKNOWLEDGMENTS

I wish to thank The W. E. Upjohn Institute for Employment Research for encouraging the initiation of this study, and for the financial support which made it possible. Editorial assistance by Judith Brawer of the Institute staff was invaluable.

I am indebted to New Ways to Work, which, as a community resource center focusing on employment counseling and social change, has provided an atmosphere in which job seekers feel comfortable. In the past five years, about a third of these clients were looking for more flexible job arrangements. Many found them through the Center's assistance. The New Ways to Work program in job sharing began informally in 1973 with local efforts in school districts and city government. It then developed under CETA funding for a special pilot project in 1975-76 and is now continuing under the auspices of several San Francisco foundations. Because of its pioneering program, one of several at the Center, New Ways to Work has become a national clearing house for information on job sharing. The directors of the many state and local government and private projects have reciprocated by providing information during the process of this study.

Several New Ways to Work staff members contributed to the preparation of this study. Zahava Rosenblatt helped with the original questionnaire design; Willie Heller and Marcia Markels interviewed many participants. Barney Olmsted reviewed the manuscript during its process. Sigrid Ruggels was responsible for the initial proofreading.

Matilda Butler of the Stanford University Department of Communications assisted in the survey instrument and analysis of the data, together with Kay Magill and Cheryl Parry, also at Stanford. Emily Nadeau typed many revisions and special thanks are due Jean Garrett for her competent and cheerful secretarial aid throughout the study.

Above all, I wish to thank the participants of the survey, particularly those who were interviewed. They gave generously of their time—no small matter in light of their reasons for becoming job sharers.

Facts and observations expressed in the study are the sole responsibility of the author and do not necessarily represent positions of the W. E. Upjohn Institute for Employment Research.

Gretl S. Meier

*Palo Alto, California*
*December 1978*

# CONTENTS

# TABLES

# Chapter One

# Perspectives: The Evolution of Job Sharing

Job sharing has evolved as a way to increase the opportunities for career part time employment. This chapter first indicates the trends in the last decade which have stimulated interest in greater work flexibility, generally, and in job sharing in particular. It then summarizes such initiatives to implement change as legislation and early experimentation, and reviews the patterns of ad hoc arrangements. By pointing to the issues posed in attempts to form policy, the recent past may put the future in perspective.

## CHANGING DEFINITIONS

Because old words often hide new meanings, vocabulary needs clear definition. The term "job sharing" is both new and old. For some readers it implies the poverty sharing during Depression years, for others the type of sharing experienced during the labor shortage of World War II. As the term is now used, "job sharing" comes from efforts in the late sixties to develop new career level opportunities in part time jobs by restructuring full time, 40-hour week positions.

A newly developed hybrid just beginning to show its shape, the arrangement has been called sharing, splitting, pairing, twinning, and tandem employment. As yet there is little agreement on terminology, even among practitioners. Job sharing is generally taken to refer to a *way to convert* full time jobs into two or more part time positions—often without regard to *how* jobs are divided.

As the concept is put into practice, however, it means either a horizontal division, where both employees are equally responsible for total job requirements, or a split, where jobs are divided vertically and each employee is responsible for a distinct half. We use the term generically, to mean *an arrangement whereby two employees hold a position together, whether they are as a team jointly responsible for the whole or separately for each half.* Basic criteria are that it: 1) is voluntary—an option chosen by the worker; 2) involves the deliberate conversion of a full time position; 3) depends on the existence of a partner or other half; and 4) includes provision of fringe benefits. Whether jobs created by division are different *in nature* from all part time jobs will be discussed in later chapters.

Job sharing is related to part time work and to work sharing, or as it is now being called, "leisure sharing," but it differs distinctly from both. Although all shared jobs are less than full time, not all permanent part time jobs are created by restructuring positions for two partners. (Nor, it should be added, does collaboration exist only in shared job arrangements. Obviously, many full time workers often informally share tasks with others in the organization. The point is that collaboration is more likely to be a *requisite* in shared jobs than in other work arrangements.)

"Work sharing" is a measure to reduce work time on a percentage basis for *all* employees or a segment of employees within a firm, as an alternative to a layoff of a corresponding percentage of its work force. Usually a temporary measure, work sharing has traditionally been a management initiative, though moves are now being made to explore this as a possible voluntary solution to unemployment.

Such situations may encourage creation of individual job sharing opportunities, but only insofar as they allow genuine freedom of choice for each worker. These distinctions, although not yet clear, are important because job sharing, part time work, and work/leisure sharing are often discussed together with other forms of flexibility, including flextime and the four-day work week. All of these changes come primarily from the increasing awareness of the need to fit work to the worker. Job sharing is one specific alternative.

## EARLY EXPERIMENTS

One of the early experiments in restructuring full time positions which began in the late sixties was a Professional and Executive Corps initiated by the Department of Health, Education, and Welfare in 1968. This program, which established new part time positions for 40 women, was never institutionalized, probably because of the complex personnel ceiling system regulated by the Office of Management and Budget. While the Corps' participants had specifically rejected partnership jobs (the speculation being that matching experience levels might be too difficult in administrative positions), its report recommended that agency heads consider its usage in operational or direct service jobs.[1]

In another experiment at about the same time, the Massachusetts Department of Public Welfare hired 50 women, converting 25 social worker positions. Organized by Catalyst, the New York organization founded to create new patterns of employment for college educated women, this project was evaluated as successful in terms of productivity and employee satisfaction. The project report, however, did not use the term "job sharing" nor did it elaborate the ways participants worked together.[2]

It was not until 1973 that the same organization, which by then had begun to form a national network of affiliated women's

---

1. For a discussion of the temporary nature of the Corps see Elsa A. Porter, "General Comments on Part-Time Employment. Implementing Alternative Work Patterns: Some Public and Private Sector Experiences with Flexible Working Hours and Part-Time Employment." Conference Summary of the Public Sector Session, Conference on Alternative Work Patterns, Washington, D.C., April 8, 1976 (mimeo). For a summary of Corps' experience and recommendations, see Marjorie M. Silverberg and Lorraine D. Eyde, "Career Part Time Employment: Personnel Implications for the Department of Health, Education, and Welfare Professional and Executive Corps," *Good Government,* Fall 1971, pp. 14-15.

2. Catalyst, *Part-Time Social Workers in Public Welfare* (New York: Catalyst, 1973). A few examples of partnership teaching were reported in an earlier study. See Catalyst, *Part-Time Teachers and How They Work* (New York: Catalyst, 1968).

groups, set forth a position paper defining job sharing, pairing, and other forms of part time work, and explaining the advantages of the new arrangements for employers. It also published a paper subtitled, "How to Determine and Compute an Equitable Benefit Package at No Extra Cost to the Employer" as a guide for women seeking permanent part time employment.[3]

In the decade since 1968, there has been a burgeoning of attention to various work flexibility schemes including flextime, the compressed work week and sabbatical leaves. The part time work force, in particular, has expanded considerably. Whereas in 1970 one of every eight workers was a part timer compared with one of ten in the early 1960s, estimates today are closer to one in every five and a half workers, the large proportion voluntary. The number of people looking for part time work has increased over the last ten years by an estimated three and a half million or more.[4] Moreover, the numbers of discouraged workers who have given up looking for such work, and who might not be included in these figures, cannot be determined. As Senator Nelson pointed out during the 1976 Congressional hearings on alternative work patterns, "The people we are talking about are not isolated hypotheticals who are directly affected. It is the housewife, whose children are no longer at home, the welfare mother who wants to support herself by working part time, or the older worker who feels compelled to work but on a more flexible time schedule."[5]

---

3. See Catalyst, *Flexible Work Schedules* (New York: Catalyst, 1973); and Catalyst, *Employee ("Fringe") Benefits and Permanent Part-Time Personnel* (New York: Catalyst, 1973).

4. Carolyn Shaw Bell, "Remarks from Massachusetts Part Time Employment Video Tape," Department of Personnel Administration, Commonwealth of Massachusetts, Boston, October 1977 (mimeo). See also Jerry Flint, "Growing Part Time Work Force Has Major Impact on Economy," *New York Times,* April 12, 1977, pp. 1, 56. For latest statistics, see *Permanent Part Time Employment: An Interpretive Review* (Springfield, VA: National Technical Information Service, 1976, pp. 4-7; and *Permanent Part Time Employment: The Manager's Perspective* (Springfield, VA: National Technical Information Service, 1976).

5. U.S. Congress, Senate, "Changing Patterns of Work in America, 1976," Hearings before Senate Subcommittee on Employment, Poverty, and Migratory Labor, 94th Congress, 2nd Session, 1976, p. 2.

We would suggest that the potential constituency for flexible work hours and conditions may be even more varied in light of continuing social trends. Advocates for flexibility point to the fact that the rationale for the standard work week has broken down because of changes in the nature of work and the needs of employers. With the majority of the labor force now employed in white collar and service sectors, the degree of standardization originally mandated by the manufacturing sector is no longer essential.[6]

However equivocal they may be, recent data on job satisfaction indicate not only the need for more jobs, but an undercurrent of the changing cultural expectations of work, i.e., not just any work under any conditions. These attitudes are summarized under the rubric of a sense of "entitlement."[7] Men as well as women are becoming affected by changes in family life, a younger or more educated population is questioning the traditional life cycles of education, work, and leisure and is seeking a better balance between work and the rest of their lives.

TRENDS STIMULATING WORK FLEXIBILITY

*Women in the Labor Force*

The demand by women for equal participation in the labor force, "the single most outstanding phenomenon of this century," in the much quoted phrase of Eli Ginzburg, Chairman of the National Commission for Manpower Policy, is the most obvious force for change. As women keep trying to break occupational stereotyping at all levels, so too are they demanding new work schedules. Women have always been more willing to trade income for leisure, but their increasing participation and demands for equal opportunity and equal pay have intensified the quest for part time work which is legitimately recognized as career level,

---

6. John D. Owen, "The Long Run Prospects for Alternative Work Schedules." Paper prepared for Hearings cited in footnote 5 above, pp. 476-478.

7. For a recent discussion of these trends, see Rosabeth Moss Kanter, "Work in America," *Daedalus,* Winter 1978, pp. 47-48.

carrying fringe benefits and job security. Many of those already employed are feeling the stress of continuing work at full time schedules. Those seeking entry or re-entry are no longer satisfied with jobs or with working hours as traditionally defined.

"Full time work is defined as the amount of time men ordinarily work," declared Carol Greenwald, Massachusetts Commissioner of Banks, one of the most articulate proponents of part time work for professionals.[8] Testifying before the Congressional Joint Economic Committee, she noted the usual objections that supervisory jobs are considered unsuitable for part time hours. The question becomes whether input is a necessary measurement of output or whether its importance varies for different kinds of professional work. Part time employees are often considered less efficient, as she and many others observe, because of the confusion between career oriented employees who work less than full time with office temporaries who have no long term commitment to a particular job. Moreover, the issue now posed is whether part time work should be identified with women's work.[9]

## Family Changes

All too often discussed as a women's problem, reduced work schedules need, instead, to be considered as a concern of men, women and children, and of society as a whole. Because two earner families are now the predominant form of family life in the U.S., some analysts concerned with the future of America's

---

8. The definitions and remarks in this section are discussed in Carol S. Greenwald, "Part-Time Work: Is It Legitimate for Men and Women." Speech prepared for Joint Economic Committee of U.S. Congress, October 7, 1976 (mimeo).

9. It should be added that although the proportion of women in part time jobs is higher than the proportion of men, the numbers of men and women employed only part-time are similar. Recent statistics show a growth in the numbers of young and older men (compared with women, who span all age categories). Year round part time employment shows little increase as a proportion of total part time employment; however, proportionately more prime age men work year round than part year (6 months or more) compared with young and older men, whereas year round part time is greater for women in middle age than younger years. See Hilda Kahne and Andrew I. Kohen, "Economic Perspectives on the Roles of Women in the American Economy," *Journal of Economic Literature,* December 1975, pp. 1278-1279. For data on participation by men in part time labor force see *Permanent Part Time Employment: An Interpretive Review,* pp. 3-9.

children are examining the importance of flexible work schedules for both parents. Until very recently it has been assumed that, mothering being more important than fathering, it is the working wife who should take a part time job when children are young. Demands for policy measures permitting parental leave time (as in Sweden and France) are voiced rarely in this country. However, the question being raised is whether the right to work and the right to care for children might be the same for both parents if more part time work options were available. In a few instances in the U.S. and elsewhere, married couples are choosing to create their own solutions by sharing the same job. Whatever the motivation for men's interest in more flexible work time, the strain on family life when two-thirds of all mothers are working full time, is causing re-examination of rigid work schedules.

A recent preliminary study on the stresses and supports in family life offers the tentative finding that the greatest concern of parents of young children is the inflexibility of their work.[10] It indicates that in "intact" families, the highest stress for mothers arises when working full time, less when not working at all, but *least* when working part time. This same group reports greater satisfaction, not only in relation to their jobs but in their sense of adequacy as parents and in their positive attitudes toward their children. It clearly implies that part time work opportunities may be a means of helping to preserve the family unit.

In single parent families (now 13 percent of all families) the need for part time work, especially at higher paid jobs, becomes even more crucial. The same study notes that for women who are heads of households, stress is least *only* for those who work part time in the highest occupational levels; otherwise, work only adds to frustration.

This suggests that flexibility of work schedules would help at least those families who have sufficient income. For many, flexible

---

10. For discussion of the study, see statement by Urie Bronfenbrenner, Hearings of the Subcommittee on Employee Ethics and Utilization of the Committee on Post Office and Civil Service, on H.R. 1627, H.R. 2732, and H.R. 2930, 95th Congress, 1st Session, May 24, 26, June 29, July 8, and October 4, 1977.

work schedules are financially possible with one and a half salaries. For the single parent, male or female, sufficient income might depend on the availability of part time work at higher salary levels.

## Young Workers

Traditionally, younger workers, as a group, have been among those preferring part time work. What will be the effect of their increasing numbers seeking entry into the labor market? They will have higher educational attainments than ever before if, as predicted, one of every four in the U.S. will hold a college degree by 1990.[11] Evidence shows the heightened expectation of work among all young workers. It also shows the changing ratio between their expectations and the availability of jobs presumed to require high levels of education and offering a high degree of creative rather than routine tasks.

Given the current inability to find enough "meaningful" jobs, some of the overqualified or overcredentialled young workers might consider part time work if it were to offer challenging tasks at decent wages, or, conversely, less time spent on dull, repetitious duties. Despite the recent tight job market, some young workers still dispute the emphasis on quantity rather than quality of work. Even if most have "mainstream" attitudes toward jobs, they distinguish between the need for order in society, the authoritarian work setting, and work with extrinsic rewards only. They are among the most likely to differentiate between "a job," as such, and their "life's work."[12]

---

11. Denis F. Johnston, "Education of Workers: Projections to 1990," *Monthly Labor Review,* November 1973, p. 23.

12. *Work in America,* Report of a Special Task Force to the Secretary of Health, Education, and Welfare (Cambridge, MA: M.I.T. Press, 1973), pp. 44-51. David C. MacMichael, "Occupational Bias in Formal Education and Its Effect on Preparing Children for Work," in *Work and the Quality of Life: Resource Papers for Work in America,* edited by James O'Toole (Cambridge, MA: M.I.T. Press, 1974), pp. 289-296. Harold L. Sheppard and Neil Q. Herrick, *Where Have All the Robots Gone? Worker Dissatisfaction in the 70s* (New York: The Free Press, 1972), pp. 113-143.

Increasing awareness of the difficulties in the transition from school to work may further dramatize the need for part time work opportunities. A few colleges have work-study programs, but more attention is now directed to the needs of high school students. A recent program at an Illinois bank in which 500 teenagers worked half time was deemed so successful by management that it suggested a second shift of students might be added to share full time jobs.[13] Indeed, the whole traditional separation between the worlds of education and work into narrow time periods is being scrutinized.

Part time work for many students has always existed, but with the rising costs of higher education and declines in enrollment, administrators may seek to actively encourage more part time students. Part time students will need flexible work schedules.

## Life Cycles, Education, Work, Retirement

Redistributing work over the work year and over the life span is receiving increasing consideration. Both the movement for early retirement and for extension of retirement age suggest recognition of the desirability of broader flexibility. The Social Security Act recently passed may also generate more demand by retirees.[14] New suggestions point to the importance of changing the "lock-step" linear life pattern in which the early years of education are followed by the middle years of work life and later years of leisure. The accepted cycle frustrates retirees and the young, as well as those of prime age who would conceivably choose more leisure at that time if it were possible to do so without sacrificing job status completely. It has been proposed that a more "cyclical" life plan would define alternating periods of work and non-work over the course of one's life by such means as flexible patterns which would

---

13. "Continental Bank: Young Workers Mark Success of Work-Study Plan," *World of Work Report,* June 1977, p. 65.

14. The Social Security Act passed in 1978 will raise to $6,000 (by 1988) the ceiling for income earnable without charge against Social Security benefits for persons 65-70 years of age. For this reason, part time and shared positions in this salary range may become more attractive for the retirees.

permit extended leaves of absence, sabbaticals, work sharing and individual job sharing arrangements.[15]

Part time work, be it part year or part week, has a likely role in such a pattern, a role not yet explored but suggested later in this study. The pairing of older workers into restructured jobs is one such possibility. The pairing of workers of different ages in an apprentice-type arrangement, already apparent in some individual job sharing situations, merits attention. Organizations which will be exempted from extended retirement, such as institutions of higher learning, are among those which might make best use of job sharing.

Economic policy needs as well as social or philosophical considerations motivate discussion of changing life cycles. Reducing work time as an alternative to high unemployment is once again being raised as a broader issue than individual job sharing.[16] If the increase in part time work is to be justified as an employment creation measure, it will surely need to be promoted on a much larger scale. This may force further examination of trends already noted, to determine how pervasive is the desire for a time-income exchange and how inhibiting are government regulations and collective bargaining agreements. Evaluation of this rationale, however, remains premature at this time. Although job sharing may some day become a valid means of creating more full time positions, this cannot be viewed realistically as a primary purpose of the option.

---

15. Juanita Kreps, "New Strategies for Education, Work and Retirement in America." Remarks prepared for the Conference on Life Cycle Planning for Full Employment, Washington, D.C., April 21, 1977. Fred Best and Barry Stern, "Education, Work, and Leisure: Must They Come in That Order?" *Monthly Labor Review,* July 1977, pp. 3-10.

16. Peter Henle, *Work Sharing as an Alternative to Layoffs* (Washington, D.C.: Congressional Research Service, 1976). Sar A. Levitan and Richard S. Belous, "Reduced Work-Time: An Alternative to High Unemployment?" Conference on Job Creation sponsored by the National Council for Employment Policy and Michigan State University, May 19, 1977. "Leisure Sharing," Hearings of the California Senate Select Committee on Investment Priorities and Objectives, Sacramento, 1977. Robert Clark, *Adjusting Hours to Increase Jobs,* special report 15 (Washington, D.C.: National Commission for Manpower Policy, September 1977).

The recent efforts to promote job sharing will suggest that individual efforts are in fact expanding. However, whether job sharing is an idea whose time has come, or whether it will be a long time in coming, if ever, will depend on how the complications it engenders are mastered. Is it work or the worker who will really change? A review of experiments in promoting flexible opportunities indicates both the potential advantages and difficulties ahead.

## POLICY INITIATIVES AND IMPLEMENTATION

### GOVERNMENT EMPLOYEES

#### *Policy at the National Level: Current Status*

The most identifiable initiatives to implement changes are the efforts to legislate flexible working hours for government employees. Government needs to increase *all* measures to create employment opportunities, but at the same time has a special role in initiating and encouraging use of alternative patterns. Some advocates for expanding permanent part time opportunities point out that the private sector is not likely to generate sufficient openings because of both real and imagined costs, and because of lack of appreciation of potential benefits. It has often been suggested that legislation be enacted which would lower relative costs of alternative work schedules by such means as wage subsidies or tax credits for firms who increase the number of nonstandard work schedules. It has also been proposed that the relative costs of other forms of government subsidy, such as child care facilities, should be measured against the cost of implementing alternative work schedules.[17] As a major employer, government is called on to take the lead and to develop information through demonstration projects.

Policy initiatives at the federal level include a recently drafted Civil Service Commission plan prompted by an executive directive and a Congressional bill which has been in process several years.

17. Isabel Sawhill, remarks at Hearings cited in footnote 5, p. 472.

During the presidential campaign, President Carter stated:

I will encourage—actively and aggressively—the adoption in the Federal government and in the private business sector, of flexible working hours for men and women, and I will take action to increase the availability of part time jobs, with proper provision for fringe benefits and job security.[18]

The budget message for fiscal year 1979, which contains provision for experiments within five federal agencies, carries through an earlier executive directive that the Civil Service Commission draft action plans to develop such a program. In order to utilize existing agency employment ceilings, the Commission is to report by April 1979 on policy changes required for implementing in fiscal year 1981 conversion of regular positions on the basis of the fraction of hours worked (i.e., full time equivalents) rather than the numerical "head count" now in use.[19]

The need for this change to fractional ceilings has been one of the barriers to passage of currently pending legislation whose initiatives began in 1973.[20] A part time bill was approved by the Senate in 1975, but its companion House measure was never reported out of committee. In the following year, the Senate Committee on Labor and Public Welfare subcommittee hearings on alternative work patterns included discussion of flextime, part

---

18. *Congressional Record* (daily edition), January 31, 1977, p. S-1738.

19. The draft plan calls for demonstration projects and outlines concurrent research and demonstration programs to test part time employment. See *Civil Service Bulletin*, No. 312-314, and attachments, December 5, 1977. The agencies named are: Veterans Administration, Federal Trade Commission, Environmental Protection Agency, General Services Administration, and the Export-Import Bank. Kathy Sawyer, "Proposed Program Aimed at Increase in Permanent Part-Time Federal Jobs," *Washington Post,* January 24, 1978, p. A12.

20. The first bill (S-792), "Career Part Time Employment," introduced by Senator Tunney in June 1973, was revised as "Flexible Hours Employment" (S-2022). The legislation before the 95th Congress, 1st Session, is entitled "Part Time Employment" (H.R. 10126, revised from H.R. 1627), sponsored by Rep. Burke, and the earlier Senate version is S-518. For discussions of the Tunney bill see "Flexible Hours Employment," Hearings before the Senate Committee on Post Office and Civil Service on S-2022, 93rd Congress, 1st Session, September 26, 1973. For discussions of the pending legislation, see Hearings, cited in footnote 10 above.

time and job sharing. "Part Time Opportunities in the Federal Government," the most recent bill, was introduced by Senator Nelson in January 1977. The companion House bill (Rep. Burke) was discussed (together with bills on flexible hours and compressed work week) at hearings in May 1977 and again in January 1978. The latest revisions were accepted by the House Committee on Post Office and Civil Service early in February, and the bill was approved by the House in March.[21]

Over the years, sponsors have reiterated the need to increase part time positions beyond the number and low levels to which they have been limited.[22] The legislation speaks of the productive potential of older workers, handicapped, students, and parents, unused because of standard working hours. It notes the benefits to government as employer of increasing productivity and job satisfaction, and to society of offering an alternative to those who prefer shorter hours (in spite of reduced income), thereby increasing jobs available to reduce unemployment and still retain skilled workers.

H.R. 10126 defines part time work as between 16-32 hours, with equal or varied daily schedules, whether part time or established by job sharing, but excluding temporary or intermittent employment. It changes the method of determining personnel ceilings referred to earlier. It directs agencies (with certain exclusions) to promote part time opportunities up to Grade 16 after positions become vacant, and specifically prohibits the creation of positions by abolition of occupied positions where it would be necessary to force full time workers to choose between part time work or none at all. In addition, the bill specifies

---

21. This bill was approved by the Senate and signed by President Carter October 10, 1978.

22. *Congressional Record,* 93rd Congress, 1st Session, June 19, 1973, *Congressional Record,* 94th Congress, 1st Session, February 1, 1975, and *Congressional Record,* 95th Congress, 1st Session, January 31, 1977. According to a 1973 survey by the Civil Service Commission, part time positions are concentrated in grades GS-7 and below; most are temporary, provide fewer fringe benefits and are held predominantly by persons under 21 years of age. See "Part Time Employment in Federal Agencies." Report to the Congress by the Comptroller General of the U.S. Civil Service Commission, Office of Management and Budget, Washington, D.C., January 1976, pp. 3-6.

non-applicability where collective bargaining agreements establish the number of hours of employment and recognizes entitlement of existing employee organizations to represent part time employees.

The Civil Service Commission, which is to establish and maintain programs at the request of agencies, is also directed to conduct a research and demonstration program: 1) to determine the extent to which part time employment may be used in positions traditionally not extensively open to such arrangements, i.e., supervisory, managerial and professional; 2) to determine where job sharing positions may be established; and 3) to evaluate benefits, costs, efficiency and productivity as well as its "various sociological effects as a mode of employment."

The significant change from earlier bills is the substitution of the term "annual goals" for establishing or converting positions, in lieu of a progressive 2 percent annual quota until 10 percent is reached in five years. This had been opposed by the Civil Service Commission and others on the grounds that it called for a cumbersome system of waivers and would undermine the merit system in favor of "special interest groups." Spokesmen for the American Federation of Government Employees and National Federation of Federal Employees opposed the bill, stating that the number of slots should be a negotiable item rather than a quota, and that fragmentation into part time positions jeopardizes full time slots and promotion for full time workers.[23]

However, it appears at this time that executive action, favored by the Carter administration, may supersede the implementation of the legislation. The Civil Service Commission has long claimed that a new law is unnecessary, and that administrative authority exists for expanding part time opportunities. The Office of Management and Budget has opposed the changes in personnel ceilings called for in earlier Congressional bills. Moreover, progress in implementing legislation at the state level indicates that the actual creation of part time positions does not necessarily occur except where such laws provide for specific demonstration projects.

---

23. Hearings cited in footnote 10 above, pp. 63, 170.

## Experience in State Governments

Efforts to increase alternative work schedules at the state government level also began in the mid-seventies. Although at the present time 20 states are reported to have fashioned some type of new work time arrangements, most are within the 40-hour week framework and result from administrative mechanisms. Recent years have seen new proposals for legislation to increase part time opportunities, often including the job sharing option. Several are in the introductory stage only. In New York, for example, the Department of Civil Service is to determine feasibility and assist in implementation, with a targeted progressive quota of 10 percent.[24] The State of Washington has held hearings on a measure which is similar, but more closely patterned on the latest federal bill. Hawaii has prepared an extensive feasibility study in an attempt to generate cost data in order to formulate possible legislation.[25]

Oregon enacted legislation in October 1977, directing its Budget and Management Division to encourage job sharing with prorated fringe benefits for state employees, and to report to the 1979 legislative session on the extent of its use.[26] Like the latest federal

---

24. *An Introduction to Alternative Work Schedules and Their Application in the State of New York.* Prepared by the Temporary State Commission on Management and Productivity in the Public Sector, February 1977. Molly Ivins, "Bill in Albany Asks for Flexible Work Time," *New York Times,* March 13, 1977, p. 45.

25. *The Feasibility of Job Sharing by Public Employees in Hawaii,* Legislative Reference Bureau, State of Hawaii, July 1977. In the State of Washington, a random sample of state employees and agency directors indicated that a majority favored the introduction of some form of part time arrangements. See "Preliminary Results from Part-Time Employment Survey." Memorandum from the Office of Program Research, House of Representatives, Olympia, Washington, November 15, 1977 (mimeo). "Part-Time Permanent Employment: A Review of Background Material." Memorandum from the Office of Program Research, Olympia, Washington, August 30, 1977. The proposed legislation is embodied in House Substitute Bill 1139.

26. The Division plan to aid agencies explains in detail the intent of job sharing, personnel, and reporting procedures, and clarifies agency responsibilities. The state has initiated what appears to be an active educational program for state personnel, including assistance through a work group representing agencies which have already used or have significant potential for job sharing. A Division report identifies by agency the salary range and number of positions filled by job sharing. See Memorandum from the Executive Department on H.R. 2608, H.R. 2538, Salem, Oregon, October 1977 (mimeo).

bill, the act has been interpreted more flexibly than the 10 percent original target provision so as to encourage usage and keep reporting minimal.

That there is a hiatus between legislation and implementation is evidenced in states whose efforts have had a longer history. Maryland's legislation stipulated creation of part time opportunities with progressive quotas up to 5 percent and directed its personnel department to apprise agencies of their obligations. Its preliminary progress reports indicate problems with compliance. [27] The Massachusetts program, based on the first state level part time employment statute (1974), illustrates some of the difficulties.

### Massachusetts

Prior to legislative action, part time employment in Massachusetts, as in other states, had been possible but was seldom encouraged. Most part time positions resulted from individual employee requests or labor shortages in specific job titles and are found in few of the 27 major state agencies. In spite of the successful 1968 experiment in the Department of Public Welfare referred to earlier, little effort was made to replicate the experience, even with the advent of the 1974 law. Patterned on the first federal bill, that legislation includes position percentage goals, prorated benefits, and a broad span of job titles and grade level positions. However, the hiring of a Flexible Hours Coordinator charged with assisting implementation was not approved until November 1976, after establishment of a demonstration flextime program. Original delays are attributed to 1975 fiscal crises and department reorganization of the administrating agency. [28]

---

27. *Report on Part Time Employment in Maryland State Government,* August 1976 (mimeo); and *Report to the General Assembly, Part Time Positions,* January 1977, Maryland Department of Personnel (mimeo).

28. *Rationale for the Part-Time Program Policy: Flexible Part-Time Project—April 1977 Progress Report,* Boston, Office of Coordinator of Flexible Hours, Division of Personnel Administration (mimeo); "Job Sharing in the Public Sector," Conference sponsored by New Ways to Work, Inc., San Francisco, March 2, 1978 (to be published).

The slow rate of implementation in 1977, according to Massachusetts Department of Personnel staff, was due to the widespread lack of appreciation for advantages to management coupled with traditional resistance to administrative complications, and to the existence of a collective bargaining agreement negotiated prior to the part time benefits regulations. Since the agreement incorporated benefits for part timers based on policy developed prior to the enactment of the 1974 statute, salary increment and vacation leave were inadequately provided. Securing an amendment to the collective bargaining contract proved to be an extraordinarily complicated process. Major accomplishments to date include development and promulgation of regulations defining benefits and civil service procedures for part time employees, documentation of current percentages of part time positions by grade level and agency, and production of a video tape explaining the management advantages of the part time option.

Looking ahead, the agency foresees that the filling of vacant positions as they arise, either by job sharing or part time employees, is less likely to occur than the voluntary reduction of hours by full time employees. Anticipated union objections to the former, which would withhold positions from unemployed full time applicants, are unlikely with the latter, which would provide new alternatives to the current work force and open new part time jobs to unemployed applicants.

Programs in two other states, Wisconsin and California, illustrate some of the same difficulties but also show the efficacy of different approaches.

*Wisconsin*

Wisconsin's Project JOIN (Job Options and Innovations) is a more directed research and demonstration project. It is supported by federal funds to cover staff and training reimbursement to the state in order to secure jobs, and by the state (contributions in kind) to cover wages and fringe benefits for participants. The two-year project was initiated in 1976 with the goal of transforming a minimum of 25 permanent full time professional and para-professional civil service positions into 50 jobs. It was designed to measure productivity and the effects of shared positions on full time workers in the same units; determine specific characteristics of persons seeking shared jobs; develop material for project replication; and research retirement laws to determine impediments.

JOIN's several reports indicate progress and specific problems.[29] The project had assumed that users would be primarily women, the handicapped, and older workers. It was hypothesized that persons nearing retirement would choose to reduce hours, and that some would return to work on a reduced schedule. To date, women make up 76 percent of the participants; however, the average age is 34, and only 13 percent of the participants are over 40. Hiring of both older workers and the handicapped has been difficult. The project's *Retirement Law Survey* reviews the barriers in current retirement laws for older workers who want to reduce their hours.

More important, however, although the number of positions identified for conversion (44) surpasses the project's goal, the process of filling positions has proved extremely slow. JOIN indicates that the initial commitment of positions was complicated by supervisory attitudes including stereotypes of part time employment, consideration of costs, additional supervisory work, and administrative problems such as payroll. Since normally Wisconsin Civil Service prohibits two people from applying for one position, each half of the shared position had to be recruited and hired individually. Conversions were easiest where incumbents wanted to reduce to half time (only 10 of the 44 positions were vacant). In some instances they were paired in one job and in others a vacant half was filled from outside Civil Service. Thirty of the 81 participants were new to Civil Service.

---

29. *Project JOIN—A Demonstration to Develop and Test Job Sharing in Wisconsin Civil Service,* Phase I Report, May 1, 1977, Phase II Report, and Quarterly Report, September 30, 1977. *Project JOIN—The Effect of Part Time Employment on Retirement Benefits,* Madison, State Bureau of Human Resource Services, November 18, 1976 (mimeo).

JOIN reports favorable attitudes among supervisors and participants during progress of the experiment, but points to particular on-the-job complications. Initial work schedules were changed to accommodate time for follow-up (i.e., half days to some full days). In positions where supervisors were wary of part time arrangements because of the need for continuity, it was found that the best schedules were four days at five hours per day or half days, and six months on and off. Civil Service regulations, however, made the half year alternative more difficult because of unforeseen problems in prepayment of health insurance, status during non-work time, and eligibility for unemployment compensation. The measurement of compensatory time, another initial problem, appeared to be solved by more specific communication with supervisors.

JOIN emphasizes the continual need for supervisory and co-worker support to preclude the likelihood of co-worker resentment and charges of favoritism toward sharers, as well as to provide advance preparation for union representatives.

Promotional opportunities under existing rules are limited because of regulations on the accrual of time. In some areas, sharers have been accorded full seniority, but in reclassification and promotion they are only given credit for hours worked. JOIN staff sees this as a problem in that the normal state probationary period for both full and part time employees is six months, but personnel offices count only that time worked.

The random selection of positions originally planned by the project was modified because it didn't allow for supervisory approval. The use of current eligibility lists hinders sharers' role in the choice of partners. Recruitment and selection, JOIN indicates, ensured complementary skills, but not compatibility of the two personalities. Of the first 40 positions filled by two employees, it appears that most if not all are separate halves; few are the joint responsibility of both partners, a possibility JOIN had envisioned for some positions. It is difficult to ascertain what measures were used to recruit complementary partners or whether the procedure of task analysis proved few jobs suitable for closer teaming. Although it is too early to fully assess the program, it is to be hoped that later evaluations will examine the particular issues involved in filling professional positions within Civil Service.

## California

One California demonstration project, initiated in 1977 to continue for two years, differs in approach from Project JOIN but has had some of the same difficulties as well as some positive results.[30] The Part Time Employment Program, a project within the State Department of Motor Vehicles designed to test creation of part time opportunities and expansion to other agencies, also includes various time schedules. It allows for choices of work time reduction from 8 to 32 hours in either shared, split, or part time arrangements.

At the present time, there have been 238 conversions or individuals hired into part time, 95 percent of whom chose half time arrangements. Although slightly over half of participants were formerly permanent full time employees in the department, a substantial number (38 percent) were former state employees in permanent intermittent positions. A smaller number (8 percent) included former state employees who returned to Civil Service to take advantage of the part time option, transfers from other agencies, and new hires from eligibility lists.

In terms of the impact of the part time option on unemployment, the report indicates the importance of these figures. Approximately 26 full time equivalent positions were created as a result of the conversions, which meant 38 new hires, both full and part time. The California report points out that if this percentage were to hold constant, approximately 400 full time positions could be created statewide if the option were extended to all Civil Service employees.[31]

Preliminary evaluation of employee and department attitudes indicates that both participants and supervisors are generally

---

30. "Report of the Legislation of the State of California: The Part Time Employment Pilot Program," First Interim Report, July 1, 1977, Second Interim Report, January 1978, Sacramento, Department of Motor Vehicles.

31. Second Interim Report, cited in footnote 30 above, pp. 1-4.

affirmative. Participants perceive the advantages in terms of personal lives, job attitudes, and motivation to work. They list as a particular disadvantage the limited upward mobility because of slower promotion rate, which accounts for a higher than average turnover rate in the department. Almost half of those no longer in the program returned to full time positions. The report notes, however, that supervisors feel that productivity of participants is as great as that of full timers. While costs have not yet been computed, there has been a decrease in use of sick leave and savings due to lower premium pay for overtime (because of slower hourly accrual rate). Increased costs come primarily from health care benefits because, under current personnel board rules, employees working over 20 hours receive full rather than prorated benefits.

Two issues raised for statewide expansion are again to be noted. The first concerns managerial understanding and willingness to support part time—especially in higher level positions. Although there is now representation in some professional and supervisorial clerical positions, the department has found it difficult to convert a great number of higher level positions. The report points to the need for employees with more experience. This, in turn, would require the availability of a wider applicant pool to ensure adequate supply (to fill in for conversions, replace leavers, and facilitate promotion of other part time employees). The lack of a separate eligibility list exclusively for applicants wishing part time positions hinders potential users of the program. The long term answer, however, according to the project director, is concurrent use of lists by full time and part time, but with credibility to the process so that potential part timers believe opportunities are truly available.

A second, shorter term project in California focuses specifically on shared positions, which are few in number in the larger Department of Motor Vehicles program. The State Personnel Board Shared Project, under a grant from the Intergovernmental Personnel Act, converted 28 positions in 13 state departments, all on a half time basis. The program was initiated in 1976, when the status of the larger program had not yet been determined. Its conversion of positions was completed a year later, and the program officially ended in March 1977.[32] The 51 individuals who shared were, for the most part, current state employees who wished to reduce time. Those employed from outside, it was felt, were individuals who preferred full time and were already on Civil Service lists. However, when a full time vacancy occurred as a result of partnering, the full time vacancy was not always filled, ostensibly because of the short term duration of the project. Over half of the positions in the total conversion were clerical, but another third (8 of 27) were technical and professional.

Both supervisors and participants evaluated the program as successful; the new arrangements either maintained or increased productivity. This was especially notable in clerical jobs, where unit production was measured on the same employees before and after the experiment. The staff noted, however, that measurement of costs proved difficult. Not only was the group limited in numbers, but costs were not well enough identified during the process of the program. The evaluation stresses the importance of adequate preplanning and control. Among the problems to be considered when replicating the project was the need to eliminate inequities to the employee (such as prorating of vacation time) and to the department, particularly a less expensive retirement system.

### The Experience in County and Local Governments

Job sharing in county and city offices has, for the most part, occurred on an individual ad hoc basis or in small scale experiments. These have increased in the last two years and include arrangements in Oregon: Land County and the City of Salem and the City of Eugene; Wisconsin: City of Madison; Washington: King County and the City of Seattle. Several offices in California have already instituted job sharing arrangements and others are now in progress.[33] The County of San Diego recently

---

32. For this discussion see "Shared Positions Project," Six Months Report, October 1976, Twelve Month Progress Report, February 1977, Sacramento, State Personnel Board.

33. See "Job-Sharing Project," Personnel Department, County of Santa Cruz, May 1977 (mimeo).

began a study of the feasibility of including job sharing; similar measures have been proposed in the City of San Jose. The County of Santa Cruz has prepared an analysis of job sharing experience and is in the process of filling the 85 allocated positions. The City of Palo Alto has used sharing for several years, its teams primarily in lower level positions but some few at the professional classification.

## A California County Example

Santa Clara County in California, which employs a total of 11,000, has had the longest experience with what are called "split-codes."[34] The option to convert to full time positions has existed since the late sixties on an informal basis and has been available for several hundred positions. Although some arrangements had existed earlier, these had generally been instituted at the behest of management, rather than employees. In 1975, the Service Employee International Union (Local 715), which represents some 75 percent of county workers, pressed for the establishment of a minimum specific number of split-codes guaranteed as an employee right. When this proved successful, it negotiated for a higher minimum (200), subject to annual review with the county.

County spokesmen explain that the administration imposes no minimum seniority restrictions and that the master union agreement has no such stipulation. The union may negotiate on behalf of individual units so that available split-codes are bid on, and the most senior workers receive split-code assignment. If there is no conflict with regulations, the county may recruit the other half of a split-code from outside. In other cases, a qualified worker must be available and interested or the original employee must return to full time. Supervisorial approval is a necessary condition after employee application. Seniority is accrued at a slower rate, but where regulated by union rules, the worker can

---

34. This discussion of local California projects is also based on interviews with project directors, on their staff reports presented at the New Ways to Work Conference cited in footnote 28 above, and on Hearings cited in footnote 16 above.

return to full time. All split-code workers maintain fringe benefits on the same basis as full time workers. Most codes have been filled in hospitals, the Department of Health, and in libraries. Employees are most likely to be social workers, nurses, eligibility workers, and clerical staff; none are in the blue collar or management positions.

It should be explained that a greater number of employees have chosen the county's Voluntary Reduced House program which was introduced in 1976 in the face of threatened layoffs. Theoretically available to all county workers, this permits various reductions up to 20 percent at six month intervals. In these arrangements, time not worked is considered leave without pay so that seniority still accrues at the same rate and the right to return to full time is guaranteed. As of this date, the county has not studied turnover, productivity, or costs for any of these schemes.

## The State of Washington

A recent short term (five and a half months) experiment on "Part Time Careers in Public Service" involved 48 part timers, some in pairs, in King County, the City of Seattle and the University of Washington.[35] Evaluation of results as measured with control groups, again, is positive, particularly in terms of efficiency and energy on the job, with less use of sick leave. However, continuity in certain jobs proved difficult, and the report stresses the need for communication among part time and full time staff.

On the basis of discussion with project staff, some further observations might be made about the problems of short term experiments. The county program was designed to include new hiring, all in pairs which were intended to be collaborative arrangements. In effect, these professional positions were split vertically, since supervisors tended to give separate assignments. In the city sites, which included both professional and

35. Final Report of Demonstration Project: City of Seattle, University of Washington, King County. Abstract, Institute of Governmental Research, University of Washington, Seattle, January 1978.

non-professional positions, some were part time, others in pairs, both separate and collaborative. It was pointed out that, in at least one instance, had the experiment continued, participants would have worked into a more cooperative arrangement (rather than as happened, with the incumbent taking more responsibility for higher level tasks). In at least two sites (county and city), participants were likely to be disgruntled employees, and inclusion in the projects was the most effective means of meeting their problem. In addition, experiments may be used as temporary budget savers, and organizations willing to cooperate only because of their short term nature.

## INITIATIVES IN OTHER PROFESSIONS

### *Medicine*

The desire for professional part time and shared jobs has not been limited to government employees, but is reflected in efforts among certain professions. One of these concerns graduate medical training. Section 709 of the 1976 Health Professions Educational Assistance Act stipulates that institutions with medical residency training programs in primary care specialties receiving federal assistance "must establish, or restructure and maintain, . . . a reasonable number of physician training positions in such programs as shared schedule positions."[36]

The major national effort to promote alternatives to traditional scheduling in Graduate Medical Education (GME) is the Harvard Reduced Schedule Residency Project. This project deliberately omits the term "part time," since that is generally taken to mean less than 35 hours per week rather than the 35-60 hours for half time in such positions. In the shared schedule for GME (the schedule required in Section 709), two physicians share one house officer position, each working two-thirds to three-fourths time

---

36. For information on the medical training program see *Reduced Schedules Residency Project Newsletters,* No. 4-9, Harvard Medical School, December 1976-May 1978. See also Eileen Shapiro, "Implications for Pre-Medical Counseling." Speech to the annual conference, American College Personnel Association, March 29, 1977 (mimeo).

and each receiving half pay, full fringe benefits, and appropriate credit for time worked. The more than half time specified ensures overlap for continuity of patient care and participation in educational activities. In view of current hospital cost containment efforts, the requirement of pay in proportion to time worked would provide a financial disincentive for such programs.

A major premise underlying the work of the Harvard project is that many of the new generation entering medicine are questioning the extraordinary time demands in their training. Men as well as women want to combine training time with other commitments—research, family, personal avocations or other medical interests.[37] Moreover, because training time is coming to be seen as a period when professional identity is formed, the need for "maintaining one's humanness" is crucial both professionally and personally. Professional concerns center on the consideration of the effect of long hours on the quality of care delivered, the sensitivity to patient needs under long periods of stress, and the educational saturation point for physicians who are being trained in a clinical setting.

Interest on the part of students and house staff has been growing, as evidenced by inquiries to the project from both men and women (about 3,000 inquiries in the past two years). Information is not yet available on the number of such positions that have been filled nationally. The Harvard group, still the nucleus for coordinating efforts and gathering information, has published its latest directory based on a survey of 1,700 hospitals with AMA accredited residency programs.[38] This directory lists 1,051 residency programs with options for reduced or shared schedule training. However, despite a not insignificant supply *and* demand, progress appears to be slow because the required application mechanism makes applying to less than full time

37. Eileen Shapiro and Shirley G. Driscoll, "Shared Schedule Graduate Medical Education," *Resident and Staff Physician,* forthcoming issue.

38. *Institutions Offering Reduced Schedule Training: Revised Listing* (Boston: Harvard Medical School, 1977).

programs almost impossible. This situation may change now that "Criteria for Compliance" for Section 709 have been issued by the Department of Health, Education, and Welfare.[39]

As compliance with the law increases and sufficient positions are established, the project intends to research the effects on individual physicians and on the quality of care delivered and education received by shared schedule residents as compared with full time counterparts in the context of costs and services to hospitals. In this way, it is felt, it may be possible to determine the optimal scheduling for training.

*Education*

Job sharing arrangements are already established in greater numbers in teaching than in other professions, particularly at the elementary school level. These are still, however, on an individual basis. Only a few districts actually promote use of the option; administrators perceive it primarily as a way to bring in new teachers and avoid layoffs at a time of declining enrollment. Isolated instances occur in many parts of the country, but are more frequently found on the west coast—in Washington, Oregon, and Alaska, and especially in the San Francisco Bay area in California.

A preliminary survey published in 1976 covered a nine county area in California, and with information gathered since, shows that the approximate number of teachers using the option fluctuates, rarely exceeding 120 pairs.[40] The study found that administrators who had allowed shared contracts were generally extremely favorable, as were the teachers themselves. It noted that district policies are not systematized concerning the provision of benefits, tenure regulations, and advancement procedures. For

---

39. Commencing July 1978, the National Resident Matching Program regularized the procedure for student applications for shared schedules by including shared schedules residency procedures in the match for first year residency positions. Under the plan, students apply as individuals and are not responsible for finding partners. See *Newsletter,* 9, May 1978.

40. *Job Sharing in the Schools: A Preliminary Survey* (Palo Alto, CA: New Ways to Work, 1976).

sharers, the principal issues concerned task division, time scheduling, unified teaching philosophy, and the need for communication. Issues confronting administrators concerned eligibility for the option, numbers permitted, and reversibility or criteria for returning to full time teaching.

Advantages to the districts centered on the high quality of shared teaching, a result of great skill diversity within a single position and sharers' increased energy and enthusiasm. Sharing also allowed the retention of experienced older teachers and made possible some new hiring. Furthermore, the pairing of two teachers at different levels of the salary scale was perceived as a potential cost saving.

Colleges and universities, which also employ a few sharers in administrative positions, are beginning to face greater demands by faculty for part time and sharing. This subject, which can be discussed only briefly, merits further study for two particular reasons. First, there are signs that, given the impetus of individual applications for sharing which comes primarily from married couples, a few institutions have considered policies to broaden the new option of less than full time teaching on a tenure basis to other faculty members. As noted earlier in this chapter, given the increasing cost of higher education, the decreasing enrollment, and the current tenure rules, administrators in educational institutions may be more inclined to consider the feasibility of job sharing.

The second reason concerns the particular issues raised by the fact that those who are seeking joint faculty appointments are likely to be married couples. This involves unique concerns and rewards, some of which are discussed more fully in chapters two and three of this study. Couples encounter more difficulty in being hired and in maintaining separate identities within an organization which is both a professional and social setting. They also face greater challenges in the more complete work life relationship. Some married academic job sharers have turned to the arrangement because of the difficulty of both finding full time positions in the same location. For many others, there is a conscious desire to work collaboratively or a need for both to work part time in order to have time for research, family life, and the sharing of child care and domestic chores. Although their numbers are not great (perhaps fifty to sixty couples have shared academic appointments), the implications of the way they have "lived" their arrangements may provide insights for the future into the nature of work and family life.

Academic institutions which have appointed job sharing couples are also few in number. None have more than four couples and most have allowed only one or two at a time. They tend to be smaller institutions, more amenable to innovation. They see the value of job sharing as a model within the educational community. Among the colleges and universities are: Smith, Wellesley, Hampshire, Mount Holyoke, and Massachusetts Institute of Technology (Massachusetts); Scripps, Pacific School of Religion, Claremont, and Stanford (California); Grinnell (Iowa); Gustavus Adolphus and Augsberg (Minnesota); Wells, William Smith, and Kirkland (New York); and Oberlin (Ohio). Very few have written policy and most have dealt with issues on an ad hoc basis. Questions focus not only on costs, but also on complications unique to academia and the married status of partners: "nepotism," departmental voting, promotion, and separate tenure tracks for each member of the couple. That these problems have been addressed even in a small number of instances, makes for the possibility of further exploring changes in traditional institutional policy.

Emerging Issues

The examination of recent experiments and experiences with alternative work patterns suggests policy issues for future consideration. *That the issues are becoming defined is, in itself, progress toward changing work patterns.* It has been said that much of personnel policy is a convenient way of doing business, not necessarily crucial but customarily unquestioned.[41] The examination of policy, itself, should not be underrated. It brings

---

41. Carol S. Greenwald, as cited in footnote 8 above, p. 9.

to the surface the judgments that must be made on how to measure costs and benefits, not only for organizations but also for society, when individuals are allowed more choice in the way they earn a living.

It is clear, however, from the number, scale, and rate of progress of these efforts, that the eight hour-five day week is still sacred, particularly for certain occupational levels. We must remember that *the aim of job sharing is not only to increase the number but also the quality of part time opportunities.* The obstacles are often the same for both. But whereas creating part time jobs proves difficult, establishing them at higher levels through sharing poses additional complications. Information on resolving these complications is still very limited. Experience points to problems of initiating experiments and to the fact that the experiments are limited by the need to work within current regulations which were developed with the traditional 40-hour week format. Significant changes must be effected in order to determine whether permanent part time and/or job sharing will become accepted practices.

Experiments, in reality, have allowed only those already within a system to participate, i.e., those workers who have shown a desire to reduce time. Projects have not yet tested the wider demand because they have not allowed for access to part time and sharing by others, especially young and older people. Women have been the primary beneficiary because they have already been employed in certain occupations. Therefore, until a larger, more varied pool of job sharers exists, it will be difficult to assess the benefits as well as the costs of the new arrangements—either to the organization or the individuals.

Current regulations which inhibit change are notable in government, but apparent in most other fields as well. They pertain first to eligibility. In some instances, recruitment for part time jobs still comes from lists of those seeking full time work. These job seekers are likely to use available part time opportunities as a means of entry only, and to change once employed. In other instances, eligibility depends on seniority regulations or practices, whether through collective bargaining agreements or, as in the case of teachers, through administrative tenure rulings.

Financial costs to the organization are slowly being measured. The fringe benefits computed on a per capita basis, particularly Social Security, inhibit the conversion of full time positions. Positions with salaries above the base for Social Security penalize employers with double costs for two employees. Since the job sharing experiments involve government workers in large numbers, many do not involve these costs. But for all employers, the cost of *health benefits* is of concern. In some instances, this coverage for part time workers has been borne by the employer as a full cost, whether for computer convenience or more rational objectives. Where this is the case, increasing the number of converted jobs becomes more expensive than it is under prorated arrangements. In the latter instances, the employer pays half the cost for the half time employee and the employee must pay the other half to obtain full coverage. Experiments have dealt with this in an ad hoc fashion, but have not yet analyzed how to affect general policy on inequities in order to establish more shared jobs.

Job sharing also challenges regulations for the accrual of promotion time and method of calculating retirement benefits. In some instances management has granted full credit to part timers, and in others permitted a proportion based on time worked. Credit for retirement pensions poses other questions. Under the Employee Retirement Income Security Act of 1974, the employer must include all employees working over 20 hours in current retirement plans. For the government as employer, adjustments which must be made are being explored in several state projects. These involve complicated computations differing for workers already within the system and those entering or re-entering Civil Service. In Wisconsin, for example, participants have been judged ineligible during short term projects. Decisions must be made on the question of which years of earning should be the determinants for benefits. Another important issue concerns unemployment insurance. State regulations vary and the problem becomes how to take into account calculating minimum periods of employment when this is a qualifying condition for benefits.

Above all, experience has shown that these regulations will not be changed or even examined elsewhere without wider acceptance of the desirability of establishing part time or shared jobs. Experiment reports call for an essential reversal of attitudes about part time work by all personnel involved in the change process. Much of the difficulty comes from the still pervasive feeling that only certain jobs are suitable and from the perception that the person unable or unwilling to work the standard work week at standard hours is a less valuable worker. Endorsement for change at the highest levels in the organization is crucial. The support of co-workers and union officials early in the change process remains equally imperative. What the reports do not point out but can be inferred from these experiences is the need for consistent leadership within the organization to continuously facilitate the complicated change process.

Organized labor has shown little inclination to assume this role. It has, moreover, objected to federal legislation and resisted some efforts in practice. In the rare instances when demands have been articulated by its members, however, a local union or teacher's group has accepted or even pressed for the option when it has been assured that it is voluntary, carries safeguards for the rights of full time workers, and provides some form of fringe benefits. It is important to remember that several unions have supported corresponding reductions in pay and hours. However, until promotion opportunities and other concerns are more clearly assured, efforts to advance job sharing are likely to remain with outside groups.

Although leadership has come primarily from lobbying by women's groups, the response comes from a more varied population whenever part time and shared jobs are seen as legitimate, i.e., available in well paying career positions. Unless these jobs are opened to conversion, there will not be sufficient numbers—qualified applicants of either sex who must have supportive, secure income—to form a readily available labor pool and provide the continuity sought by management.

Whether higher level jobs are to be opened to sharing depends, to a large extent, on more widespread awareness of the experience of specific examples. The following chapters are based on data obtained in a survey of job sharers, only a few of whom have participated in broader initiatives. In order to examine the *nature of shared jobs* rather than the *process of initiating job sharing alone,* it will be important to identify the people who have chosen to work this way, the jobs they hold and how they are arranged, and finally, the advantages and disadvantages perceived thus far.

# Chapter Two

# Survey: Patterns and Partners

This chapter summarizes the results of a survey of 238 job sharers as to their occupations and employers, their specific work arrangements and their personal backgrounds. The data are not intended as a census of all job sharers, nor are they expected to provide valid statistical estimates of the characteristics of the population. For purposes of this exploratory research, however, they do offer insights into the range of experiences with job sharing, and suggest areas for further research and systematic analysis.

Questionnaires were sent to previously identified job sharers and to those located through inquiries to organizations which had earlier requested information from New Ways to Work, to women's groups and other community centers, and to various state, county, and city personnel offices. A separate questionnaire was sent to job sharing married couples at universities and colleges. Responses were received from 65 percent of the total number sent, from both partners of 102 teams and from a single partner of 32 teams.[1] In general, returns were analyzed on an individual rather than a team or single job basis.

Obviously, not everyone responded to every question and the percentages used in this analysis are, therefore, relative

---

1. This includes two three-person teams where all responded and another in which only two individuals responded. (134 jobs)

frequencies. Total numbers for each item are indicated on the sample survey instrument. (See Appendix).

## THE JOB SHARING SITUATION

### Basic Job Demographics

Most respondents (82 percent) are working in a full time, 40-hour week job with one other person; an additional 14 percent hold positions considered more than full time. These current positions show the restructuring of traditional employment arrangements in that over half of the sample report that their jobs were formerly held by one person in a full time capacity. In addition, a substantial percentage report that they hold newly created jobs. Smaller numbers report that their jobs had been either shared previously or held part time by one person alone.

The large majority (86 percent) of those surveyed were still employed in the partnering positions at the time of the survey. Slightly more than half had been working in teams for more than one year, 13 percent of these for four years or more.

Most respondents (77 percent) report working in teams comprised of two females, with the next most common combination (19 percent) that of one male and one female. Only 4 percent are members of all-male teams. Almost none of the teams have partners who are related, but of the 7 percent who are related, most are married couples, with a few pairs of sisters or mothers and daughters-in-law.

### Occupational Categories

Occupational categories grouped from the job titles indicated by respondents include: *teachers* (26 percent), *administrators*/coordinators/program developers (25 percent), *secretaries*/receptionists/clerical workers (15 percent), *counselors*/social workers/psychologists (13 percent), and *researchers*/technicians (9 percent). The remaining 11 percent consists of such diverse occupations as editors, bank tellers, therapists, museum designers, ministers, physicians, librarians, and food service workers. This group is identified as *other* throughout this study. For purposes of identification, groups are referred to by a common name for the overall category.

## Public Contact and Supervision

In view of the occupations represented, it is not surprising that most respondents report that their jobs involved either "heavy" or "moderate" public contact (61 percent, 29 percent). The first group includes almost all counselors, most administrators, over half of the teachers and almost half of the secretaries and those in the *other* category. More noteworthy is the number of job sharers who report a supervisory role. Over a third of the respondents supervise some other employees, presumably full time workers, numbering one to five persons (26 percent of sharers); six or more persons (12 percent of sharers).

## Types of Teams

Female teams predominate in all occupations; the only groups with different team types in large numbers are administrators and counselors. For a breakdown of the percentages in each team type in each category, see Table 2-1.

Most respondents consider the job to be *shared*—partners working collaboratively (70 percent), rather than *split*—partners working independently (30 percent). Administrators and teachers in particular, are more likely to indicate that they share, whereas counselors are the only group likely to consider that they split their jobs. Researchers and secretaries are almost evenly divided between the two categories. The distinction does not relate to whether partners are in teams of two females or one male and one female. (The very small number of two-man teams are more likely to consider their jobs as split.) However, other information shows that the definition of these two categories is open to many interpretations. (See chapter three.)

## Types of Organizations and Other Sharing Teams

Although all but a small percentage of job sharers are employed by nonprofit institutions, it is important to note that 26 percent of

**Table 2-1**
**Percentage of Sharers of Each Team Type in Each Job Category**

| Job category | Female/Female | Female/Male | Male/Male |
|---|---|---|---|
| Teacher | 28 | 19 | 22 |
| Administrator | 24 | 28 | 33 |
| Secretary | 19 | 3 | - |
| Counselor | 10 | 25 | 33 |
| Researcher | 8 | 17 | - |
| Other | 12 | 8 | 11 |

*Note:* Percentage summations may not equal 100 because of rounding.

these are in the private sector, with public institutions, education, and government accounting for the rest.

Generally, teams are employed by relatively small institutions (41 percent in organizations of 1-100 employees). Twenty-nine percent of sharers work in organizations of 25 or fewer employees. Almost one-third are to be found in organizations with 101-500 employees. *No other sharing team in the organization* is reported by 41 percent of the respondents and fewer than five sharing teams by an additional 31 percent.

Teachers are generally employed in public education in middle- and larger-sized districts and more than any other group report other sharing teams (1-5 teams for 41 percent and 6-10 teams for 35 percent). Over half the administrators work for private nonprofit organizations, including educational institutions of smaller size (1-100 employees, 56 percent), and report no other sharing teams in their organizations. Counselors usually work for governmental agencies of either the smallest size (under 100) or larger agencies (101-1,000) and report no other sharers (36 percent) or 6-10 sharing teams (28 percent). About half of the secretaries are employed in governmental agencies of 101-1,000 employees and report no other teams. Researchers are most often employed in public education, 61 percent in organizations of 1-100 which may represent small institutes affiliated with universities. They also report no other sharing teams.

*Unionization*

Slightly more than half of the respondents report that their work place is not unionized. Three-fourths of the respondents report no individual union affiliation. This may reflect either the type of job held by most respondents or the nonprofit character of most employers. ( A further breakdown by job category can be seen in Table 2-2.)

Table 2-2
**Percentage of Sharers in Each Job Category Relating to Unionization**

| Job category | Organization is unionized | Respondent is a union member |
|---|---|---|
| Administrator | 29 | 6 |
| Teacher | 62 | 40 |
| Counselor | 54 | 46 |
| Researcher | 47 | 26 |
| Secretary | 55 | 9 |
| Other | 39 | 27 |

ECONOMICS OF JOB SHARING ARRANGEMENTS

*Salary*

The large majority of respondents' salaries (total for each team) is reported as under $16,500; the largest distribution (55 percent) is in the broad range of $8,500-$16,500. An almost equal proportion of sharers receive either less than $8,500 or over $16,500. Only 3 percent earn salaries above $25,000. This may be attributed to the Social Security regulations, current at the time the survey questionnaire was constructed, which penalized the employer with double costs when the total salary of the teamed employees exceeded $16,500. (The survey salary question was designed to determine how many shared positions fell above or below the then $16,500 base.) For whatever reason, few jobs in the higher salary range have been established on a shared basis. All job categories show the majority of respondents in the $8,500-$16,500 range except secretaries, 60 percent of whose salaries were below $8,500. (Table 2-3 shows the salary range distribution as it relates to type of teams.)

**Table 2-3**
**Percentage of Sharers in Each Team Type at Each Salary Level**

| Salary | Female/Female | Female/Male | Male/Male |
|---|---|---|---|
| Below $8,500 | 24 | 11 | 30 |
| $8,501 - $16,500 | 55 | 58 | 50 |
| $16,501 - $25,000 | 19 | 22 | 20 |
| More than $25,000 | 2 | 9 | - |

Salary differentials within partnerships complicate determination of whether Social Security costs to the employer are *in fact* doubled by team employment. It cannot be assumed that partners receive identical pay just because they are sharing a job. In fact, the same salary was received by only slightly more than half of respondents. Pay differentials probably reflect varying levels of experience and/or skill rather than longevity on the specific job. (For most respondents there was no relationship between equality of pay and length of time the job had been held by the team, nor between equal salary and whether the jobs are considered shared or split.) Administrators and counselors are most likely to receive equal pay, while teachers and secretaries are least likely.

Salary increases in the form of both cost of living and merit raises have been received by a large majority of respondents (73 percent). That members of some groups said they had received neither type of increase (42 percent of researchers, 24 percent of teachers and 29 percent of administrators) may reflect the temporary or irregular nature of their positions. In addition, many of these (researchers and administrators particularly) are likely to be in newly created positions.

*Fringe Benefits*

Most respondents receive fringe benefits (84 percent), either on the same basis as full time employees, prorated, or specially arranged (40 percent, 37 percent, 7 percent). It is important to note that 16 percent of the survey group reported receiving no fringe benefits, although only 2 percent indicated that benefits were not provided to any employees in the organization. Entitlement to fringe benefits is shown as it relates to the various job categories in Table 2-4.

**Table 2-4**
**Percentage of Sharers in Each Job Category According to Entitlement to Fringe Benefits**

| Job Category | Same as full time employee | Prorated | Other* | No benefits |
|---|---|---|---|---|
| Administrator | 24 | 37 | 4 | 35 |
| Teacher | 44 | 46 | 4 | 6 |
| Counselor | 52 | 15 | 11 | 22 |
| Researcher | 42 | 47 | - | 11 |
| Secretary | 45 | 26 | 16 | 13 |
| Other | 41 | 36 | 18 | 5 |

*Special partial arrangements such as retirement benefit only, all benefits except medical, or combination of pro rata and full fringe benefits.

Since entitlement to fringe benefits is seen as important in shared jobs, distinguishing them from traditional part time work, responses were analyzed to determine what factors related to benefit provision. Some of the usual determinants such as salary level, equality of pay, pay increases, and longevity on the job were found to have little bearing. For example, in terms of salary level, 77 percent of the partners who together earn less than $8,500 *do receive benefits,* while those in the $16,500-$25,000 salary level show the greatest disparity in provision of fringe benefits. Nor does equality of pay affect the securing of benefits; 69 percent of those *without entitlement to benefits* do receive equal pay with their partners, but 49 percent who receive full or prorated benefits also receive equal pay. Almost half of the respondents employed less than one year in their shared jobs receive benefits, whereas only 36 percent of the partners employed for the longer period receive these same benefits.

One important factor in the receipt of fringe benefits seems to be the nature of the employer. Individuals employed by private, nonprofit organizations are less likely to be provided benefits than those in private profit making, governmental, or educational organizations. Unionization does have some effect. If a person is neither a union member nor employed in an organization with union representation, there is a greater chance that the person does not receive benefits.

The most clear-cut distinction, however, lies in the *previous structure* of the presently shared job. If the job was originally full time, held by one person, it is more likely that it will carry full or prorated benefits. Furthermore, sharers employed in newly created jobs are likely to be entitled to benefits (only 23 percent are not). Almost one-half of those respondents whose shared job was previously considered a part time, one person position receive no benefits. (These findings are shown in Table 2-5.)

## THE JOB SHARER: PERSON AND PARTNER

### Age, Marital Status, and Education

The job sharing survey group shows a young population; three-quarters of the sharers are less than 40 years old. Almost half are in their thirties, with an additional 26 percent in their twenties. (All others are age 41 and over, with only 7 percent in the 51-65 age range.) Those in their thirties are predominantly administrators, teachers and counselors, whereas the younger age group is well represented among researchers and secretaries.

Respondents are predominantly Caucasian (94 percent), and married (81 percent). Members of female/female teams are more likely to be married (86 percent) than those in male/female teams (69 percent), or male/male teams (40 percent). More than half of the sample (55 percent) have one or two children at home between the ages of 1 and 11 years. In terms of occupations, researchers are the only group not likely to have any children at home.

**Table 2-5**
**Entitlement to Benefits**

| Job situation | Percentage of sharers in each job situation who are entitled to fringe benefits | | | |
|---|---|---|---|---|
| | Same as full time | Prorated | Other* | No benefits |
| Organization | | | | |
| Private nonprofit | 19 | 37 | 7 | 37 |
| Private profit | 29 | 24 | 18 | 29 |
| Government | 44 | 38 | 7 | 11 |
| Public education | 53 | 37 | 6 | 4 |
| Unionized organization | | | | |
| Yes | 47 | 39 | 6 | 8 |
| No | 32 | 35 | 9 | 24 |
| Union member | | | | |
| Yes | 59 | 36 | 5 | - |
| No | 33 | 37 | 8 | 22 |
| Previous structure of job | | | | |
| Full time, one person | 46 | 37 | 6 | 11 |
| Part time, one person | 19 | 25 | 12 | 44 |
| Newly created | 28 | 45 | 4 | 23 |

*Special partial arrangements such as retirement benefit only, all benefits except medical, or combination of pro rata and full fringe benefits.

Almost half of the respondents report the B.A. as their highest academic degree, with an additional one-third having attained an M.S.W., M.A., or nursing degree. Only a very few (4 percent) have received Ph.D.'s or professional degrees in fields such as medicine or law. An Associate of Arts degree, or some college, was reported by 8 percent of the survey group, and 6 percent have received only a high school diploma.

*Partner Similarities and Differences*

There are some interesting similarities and differences in age and educational levels *within partnerships*.[2] In almost half (44

---

2. The data in this section are based on responses from 100 pairs.

percent), both partners are within the same 10-year age group, but in another 44 percent, partners' ages fall within a 20-year age differential category. This suggests that there is more pairing of diverse age and experience levels (also indicated by salary differentials) than had been thought likely. There are also some differences in educational levels within partnerships. Although almost half of the teams have partners with the same college, graduate or professional degree, in a large minority of teams (35 percent), one partner has a higher academic degree, or one has a college degree and the other only a high school diploma.

## Job Levels

As part of an analysis of attitudes toward job sharing (described in chapter three), a job level code was constructed, based on the respondents' salary from the shared job together with their level of education.[3] A comparison of job level with job categories shows that 87 percent of the secretaries are at a low level, compared with only 21 percent of counselors. Administrators, teachers, and researchers are more evenly split between high and low level jobs (54 percent, 43 percent, and 53 percent at low levels).

## Salary as Sole Income; Non-Work Time

Salary from the shared job is the sole source of family income for only 6 percent of the respondents. These included almost 20 percent of those sharers in male/female or male/male teams compared with 2 percent of sharers in teams of two females. When asked to enumerate other sources of income, 84 percent of respondents indicate spousal support and 11 percent cite another job. For this small number holding another job, slightly over half

---

3. Research literature shows that education and salary are the best indicators of job level. For instance, a person who has little education and who has a low salary is unlikely to be in a position with much authority or influence over others. A median split was used to determine low and high on the two variables. For education, low meant less than an M.A. degree and high meant an M.A., Ph.D. or other advanced degree. For salary, low meant less than $16,500 and high meant $16,501 or more. To create a new variable with an approximately equal number of persons at each level, it was specified that those who were low on both the education and salary variables were low on the job level variable, while those who were high on either education or salary or both were high on the job level variable.

indicate the need for additional income, but almost as many explain their primary reason as a "non-monetary interest."

Time not spent on the paid job is devoted primarily to performance of domestic tasks: caring for family (32 percent of mentions and caring for the home, 25 percent). Non-work time is also utilized for additional schooling (11 percent) and for recreation (18 percent).

## Previous Employment

As reported earlier in this study, most respondents were still employed in the shared job at the time of the survey. Moreover, the majority (65 percent) were already employed when they were seeking the shared job position. (Table 2-6 shows the percentage of sharers in each job category according to their prior employment status.) These observations question the general assumption that job sharing has been useful primarily as a "re-entry" mechanism. It seems, rather, that the option has appealed to those with a stable job history as well as to the long term unemployed. Most (65 percent) of the respondents had previously held full time positions; another 29 percent had held part time jobs; only 4 percent had held a shared job before. Table 2-7 and Table 2-8 show the percentage of sharers in each job category according to the type of previous employment.

It is important to note that a large proportion (60 percent) had *not* held their present shared job as a full time job. Those who *had* held their present job previously were teachers, 60 percent of whom had held the same job as a full time, one person responsibility.

The reasons respondents offer for leaving their last job concern both work time and work content. In answer to one question, 52 percent respond that part time work was a particular goal, and an additional 32 percent state a specific preference for a shared rather than part time job. In another item, respondents also offer more varied reasons; the single reason most frequently cited was to find "a more challenging job" (31 percent). Also mentioned were "care for family" (19 percent), and "change in location" (17 percent). Administrators, counselors, and secretaries are more likely to cite the first; teachers are more equally divided between change in location and family care; researchers between a more challenging job and change in location. Other reasons offered were "change in organization" (9 percent), "personal/work problems" (7 percent), "higher salary" (7 percent), and "attend school" (4 percent). Almost none of the respondents left their former job because it was terminated, but ostensibly left of their own choice.

**Table 2-6**
**Percentage of Sharers in Each Job Category According to Their Prior Employment Status**

| Job category | Employed | | | Unemployed | | |
|---|---|---|---|---|---|---|
| | Less than 1 year | 1 - 3 years | More than 3 years | Less than 3 months | 3 months to 1 year | More than 1 year |
| Administrator | 8 | 18 | 18 | 6 | 6 | 44 |
| Teacher | 2 | 18 | 67 | - | 2 | 11 |
| Counselor | 18 | 4 | 50 | 7 | 11 | 7 |
| Researcher | 12 | 29 | 24 | 6 | 6 | 24 |
| Secretary | 13 | 28 | 22 | 9 | 9 | 19 |
| Other | 13 | 35 | 22 | 9 | - | 22 |

*Note:* Percentage summations may not equal 100 because of rounding.

**Table 2-7**
**Percentage of Sharers in Each Job Category According to the Type of Their Previous Employment**

| Job category | Full time | Part time* | Free lance |
|---|---|---|---|
| Administrator | 42 | 55 | 3 |
| Teacher | 84 | 14 | 2 |
| Counselor | 48 | 52 | - |
| Researcher | 78 | 22 | - |
| Secretary | 66 | 31 | 3 |
| Other | 65 | 25 | 10 |

*Includes job sharing.

**Table 2-8**
**Percentage of Sharers in Each Job Category According to the Structure of the Job Prior to Sharing**

| Job category | Newly created | Full time 1 person | Part time 1 person | Shared |
|---|---|---|---|---|
| Administrator | 44 | 42 | 8 | 6 |
| Teacher | 7 | 82 | 4 | 7 |
| Counselor | 18 | 46 | 14 | 22 |
| Researcher | 26 | 53 | - | 21 |
| Secretary | 7 | 58 | 7 | 29 |
| Other | 27 | 59 | 9 | 5 |

*Note:* Percent summations may not equal 100 because of rounding.

## INITIATING THE SHARED JOB

As already noted, over half of the respondents report that their current shared jobs were formerly held by one person in a full time capacity. Table 2-8 shows this to be particularly true for teachers, secretaries, and the group of occupations entitled *other.* Twenty-two percent report that their jobs were newly created, with administrators and researchers figuring large in this group. Only 13 percent have jobs that had previously been shared by two or more people, primarily counselors, researchers, and secretaries.

When asked who initiated the creation of the shared job, 56 percent of the respondents report "self" or "partner." Other responses include "the organization" (29 percent) and "the union" (11 percent). It is interesting, in view of the relative novelty of the concept of job sharing, that most individuals (64 percent) said they had no unusual difficulties in creating the job. A possible explanation is that in order to combine the job skills of two different people into a coherent and salable package for an organization to consider, many of those surveyed have had to think through their abilities and job goals more thoroughly than would a single job seeker in a usual job search. It is also possible that survey research findings may not always accord with actual experience, since individual perceptions tend to vary over time.

The area mentioned most frequently as giving difficulty was "organizational personnel policy" (45 percent of mentions). Next were "salary level and its division between the two employees" (21 percent) and "the provision and prorating of fringe benefits" (17 percent). The least frequently noted difficulty was that of finding a partner (11 percent). This may be explained by the fact that over half (59 percent) of the respondents report knowing each other before working together as partners. Of the occupations, only researchers are more likely to say that they did not know partners before (68 percent); secretaries were evenly divided.

*Training*

Many respondents indicate, however, that they were not hired at the same time as their partners (60 percent report being hired separately) and that the first person hired did not train the other in applicable skills for the job. Most were trained for their positions separately. Administrators are the only sharers who seemed to be clearly hired together in any great numbers, while researchers and secretaries were usually hired separately. Table 2-9 shows this in more detail.

*Division of Responsibilities and Time*

Few respondents report difficulty in deciding how to divide responsibilities. They divide their work by time (57 percent) more than by task (27 percent), or by both (16 percent). It should be noted here that most (72 percent) consider their skills "complementary" rather than "the same" (21 percent). Administrators, counselors, and teachers are grouped in the first category (58 percent, 52 percent, 46 percent, respectively), whereas researchers and secretaries consider their skills to be more similar (47 percent, 44 percent, respectively).

An analysis of scheduling arrangements shows that most respondents (44 percent) work split weeks, i.e., two and one-half or three days, sometimes alternating in weeks; others work half days each (29 percent). Fewer have no fixed schedule (14 percent), and still fewer work with all their time overlapping (6 percent).

Secretaries are the only group more inclined to divide work by half days, while researchers most often report working without a fixed schedule. Moreover, respondents generally indicate that the partners themselves rather than the organization determine the time division. Secretaries are the only partners indicating organizational constraints affecting their arrangements.

Table 2-9
**Percentage of Sharers in Each Job Category According to Hiring and Training**

| Job category | Hired together | | First on job trained other | |
|---|---|---|---|---|
| | **Yes** | **No** | **Yes** | **No** |
| Administrator | 59 | 41 | 56 | 44 |
| Teacher | 44 | 56 | 26 | 74 |
| Counselor | 52 | 48 | 24 | 77 |
| Researcher | 21 | 79 | 43 | 57 |
| Secretary | 6 | 94 | 52 | 48 |
| Other | 44 | 57 | 36 | 64 |

*Note:* Percent summations may not equal 100 because of rounding.

## Communication

Communication between partners is a special requisite of job sharing, and 74 percent of the survey group agree with this. Administrators and teachers respond with 92 percent and 91 percent agreement, while counselors and secretaries are almost equally divided between agreement and disagreement with the need for close communication with their job sharing partner. It is interesting to note, too, that in analyzing responses from partners as teams rather than as individuals there is a great deal of similarity in answers from both partners; in 62 percent of the teams, both partners agree with the statement on need for communication time.[4]

---

4. Based on 100 teams.

Only a small number, however, report using a formal communication system such as a work log or notes, while others indicate "talking regularly" is their main method of communication. To a large extent, respondents take time outside of work for communicating with partners, although many also use overlap time at work. In response to the specific question concerning the effect of job sharing on communication with full time co-workers, only 26 percent feel this was made more difficult. Most respondents report no effect, while some indicate that communication with other employees benefited from the presence of partner teams. Researchers, secretaries, and counselors, particularly, say that job sharing has no effect on communication with other employees.

EXPECTATIONS

When asked: "Do you expect to stay in your current job as a sharer less than 1 year, 1-2 years, 3-5 years, or indefinitely," almost half indicate "indefinitely." Only 5 percent had already left or planned to leave their job in less than one year for a full time position. Teachers, administrators, counselors, and secretaries all agree strongly that they plan to stay indefinitely. Only researchers are very clear in stating that they plan to stay on for less than one year, and this may be because their jobs were designed as temporary. Table 2-10 shows that those in the youngest age group are most likely to anticipate short term employment. Reasons frequently mentioned by those who had left or planned to do so within the year are financial, wanting to work more than part time, career change, and termination of the position. Only 12 percent of the difficulties mentioned concerned the organization, 6 percent the supervisor, and 3 percent the partner.

TRENDS

As reported earlier, more than half of the respondents have been working in these restructured arrangements for longer than one year, 43 percent for one to three years, and 13 percent for more than four years. Comparison of these longer term partners with more recent sharers reveals some interesting differences. While the survey results are intended to provide only tentative baseline data, they do suggest changes in the pattern and population of job sharing which are reviewed briefly here and discussed further in chapter three.

**Table 2-10**
**Percentage of Sharers in Each Age Group According to Expected Job Tenure**

| Expected job tenure | 21 - 30 | 31 - 40 | 41 - 50 | 51 - 64 |
|---|---|---|---|---|
| Less than 1 year | 31 | 8 | 21 | - |
| 1 - 2 years | 34 | 30 | 24 | 33 |
| 3 - 5 years | 7 | 18 | 13 | 20 |
| Indefinitely | 29 | 44 | 42 | 47 |

*Note:* Percentage summations may not equal 100 because of rounding.

## Demographic Characteristics: Jobs and Sharers

More of the recent sharers are employed in full time, two person jobs than those who have been working longer. They are less likely to be in jobs that are greater than full time. This may suggest a growth in the extent of responsibilities expected or assumed by sharers over time. Another possible explanation is that recent sharers are employed in more conventional jobs. The data show that recent sharers are somewhat more likely to enter jobs which were previously held by one full time person than those who began sharing jobs earlier. Long term sharers are more likely to have come into jobs that were newly created than are recent sharers.

Whereas long term sharers are most often employed in middle-sized (101-500 employee) organizations, recent sharers are more likely to be found in both the very small (1-25 employee) *and* the large (500 or more employee) organizations. Those who have been sharers for the longer period are employed as administrators or counselors in middle-sized public service and educational organizations, while more recent sharers work as teachers and researchers in a greater variety of both the very large and very small organizations.

The recent sharers tend to be younger (21-30) than their long term sharing counterparts, who are more often in the 31-40 age range. Recent sharers are more likely to be single and a lower percentage of recent sharers have children at home than do long term sharers.

Although the numbers are still very small, only 1 percent of the longer term sharers were members of male/male teams, while 9 percent of recent sharers belong to all-male teams. (This all-male team distribution among recent sharers exceeds the overall frequency of 4 percent.)

Recent sharers depend less on spousal support than do long term sharers. This follows the marital pattern outlined above. A higher percentage of recent sharers depend instead on another job for additional income (17 percent), compared with only 6 percent of early sharers. Almost twice as many recent job sharers as long term partners cite additional income as the reason for another job.

Finally, the recently employed sharers in this survey group show a higher percentage of college and advanced academic degrees. This suggests the possibility that individuals with increasingly high educational backgrounds are considering job sharing as an alternative. Table 2-11 provides further data relating to these demographic characteristics of sharers.

*Specifics of the Arrangement*

Recent sharers are more likely to enter restructured full time jobs than long term sharers, and less likely to know their team mates before they begin working. Difficulties cited by recent sharers are largely in the areas of salary level and division, benefit provisions and prorating, *and* finding a partner. These appear to be more specific concerns than those mentioned by earlier sharers who often cite problems related to organizational and personnel policy. Apparently, as such arrangements become less novel, the more general concerns are less problematic and sharers are able to

**Table 2-11**

**Percentage of Recent and Long Term Sharers With Selected Demographic Characteristics**

| Characteristics | Recent sharers | Long term sharers |
|---|---|---|
| Job structure | | |
| Full time, 2-person job | 89 | 79 |
| More than full time job | 9 | 18 |
| Size of organization | | |
| 1 - 25 employees | 37 | 23 |
| 26 - 100 employees | 10 | 14 |
| 101 - 500 employees | 21 | 40 |
| More than 500 employees | 31 | 24 |
| Sex of team members | | |
| Male/Male | 9 | 1 |
| Female/Female | 73 | 81 |
| Male/Female | 18 | 19 |
| Age | | |
| 21 - 30 | 34 | 20 |
| 31 - 40 | 40 | 56 |
| 41 - 50 | 18 | 17 |
| 51 - 64 | 8 | 7 |
| Marital status | | |
| Single | 16 | 5 |
| Married | 74 | 87 |
| Children | | |
| Have children at home | 55 | 79 |
| Outside support from | | |
| Spouse | 74 | 91 |
| Another job | 17 | 6 |
| Reason for another job | | |
| Additional income | 61 | 38 |
| Non-monetary interest | 35 | 57 |
| Academic level | | |
| Less than college degree | 9 | 18 |
| B.A., B.S.W., Nursing | 54 | 46 |
| M.A., M.S. | 36 | 32 |

focus on specific problems involved in instituting the work situation.

Recent sharers show the same distribution of salary range as long time sharers, which is not surprising since there is a minimum of one year's time difference between the two categories. Many salary changes and innovations would not yet have been put into effect.

Almost half of those who have been on the job more than one year have received *both* a cost of living *and* a merit increase, while only 12 percent of the newer job sharers have received both. (The frequency for receiving both a cost of living and a merit increase is only 29 percent.) Not unexpectedly, 47 percent of those who have been on the job less than one year received neither a cost of living nor a merit increase, while only 9 percent of the earlier job sharers received neither. (The overall frequency for not receiving any increase is 25 percent.)

There is essentially no difference between the earlier and more recent sharers in the overall percentages of those who are entitled to benefits (whether prorated or full). It might be significant, however, that those who have been working less than one year are slightly more likely to receive full or prorated benefits than those who have been sharing jobs longer. As indicated earlier, the previous structure of the shared job appears to be the most important determinant, again suggesting that more conventional positions are being converted to shared jobs.

## Changes and Expectations

It is difficult to assess the extent to which differences in the way partners work are attributable to changes in the population and jobs, or to the dynamics of partner relationships. The respondents' written responses to open ended questions and comments in interviews tend to suggest the latter explanation. The data show, for example, that long term sharers are likely to divide their work more by task than time (31 percent), compared with recent sharers (20 percent). The time and task divisions of work, which are especially complex to report and analyze, do not appear to be related to the particular data on job category, and may instead represent a progressive accommodation in the sharing of tasks which develops with longevity on the job.

The need for communication time between partners as a team and between teams and full time employees appears to change over time. Those partners working longer as a team report fewer problems communicating with full time workers than do the recent sharers. In addition, long term partners perceive communication within the team to be less time consuming.

Significantly more of the recent partners (26 percent) expect to stay on their jobs less than one year, compared with the long term sharers, only 9 percent of whom feel they will continue for less than a year. It cannot be assumed that this finding necessarily indicates dissatisfaction with the shared job, since 23 percent of the recent sharers say they plan to leave because their positions are temporary.

Obviously, a great many factors affect the attitudes and expectations of job sharers. The next chapter will examine this complex mix of ingredients.

# Chapter Three

# Survey: Effects and Issues

To discover the effects of working in this new way—the rewards and difficulties for individuals who have deliberately chosen to work fewer hours and to earn less money—has been the primary goal of this research. The survey questionnaire produced quantitative data on sharers' attitudes, as well as comments to open-ended questions. Taken as a whole, the responses convey unmistakable enthusiasm and the perception that job sharing has been a positive and successful experience. This holds true for most of the individuals who are no longer working as sharers, as well as for those who are still so employed. Although the study does not include a quantitative measure of "job satisfaction," it would be hard to disavow the affirmative nature of most responses.

The extensive personal statements which supplement the quantitative data were in response to the following questions:

- What do you like best, least about your job?

- How are shared positions qualitatively different from nonshared jobs?

- What factors (organizational and personal) make the shared position successful, unsuccessful?

- How might the organization facilitate shared positions?

- What do you think will be the major obstacles to extending job sharing/splitting?

JOB SHARING AND WORK

The central issues for job sharers reflect the concerns of all workers: the content of the job, a sense of effectiveness, the relations with others in the work place, and the need for job security. This study, however, emphasizes the ways in which these issues are affected by the part time aspect of shared jobs and, more particularly, by the nature of partner relationships. It is first necessary to examine the meaning and value of work for job sharers. What makes these people special is that they have the opportunity to work at "real jobs," but within a time schedule of their own choosing.

*A Sense of Balance*

By far the greatest reward perceived by job sharers comes from the opportunity to balance work life with non-work time, or "with the rest of my life," as so many respondents write. It means the capacity to control the way one lives, as a wage earner and as a total social entity. Work is central in the lives of job sharers, but not the sole criterion for identity. With one or two exceptions— those who would have preferred full time jobs—the 238 individuals surveyed see this sense of balance as a result of having the ability to allocate their own time between work and other activities: time for family, children, other interests, time to "gain perspective," "to be refreshed," "time to take a deep breath and know yourself again." No numerical count can convey the effect of these repeated phrases.

"I'd be a basket case if I had to work full time; I'd also be a basket case if I didn't work at all," is a typical statement. Comments from almost every survey questionnaire express the satisfaction, the feeling of relief at having achieved a better sense of balance. "I am better at work, better at home; I can look forward to both because when I come to work I know I still have the time for other things, whereas working 40 hours at the same job can become a drag, no matter how much you like the job."

## The Kind of Work

Job sharers are people to whom having a job is important and to whom having the right job is also important. Respondents in all occupations and across all salary levels are likely to refer to characteristics of the job itself in answer to "What do you like best about your job?" They express the satisfaction of engaging in work for which they have been trained and which they find interesting, challenging, and important.

"I like the satisfaction of the chance to serve elderly people and help with their problems."

"I like helping the public, doing meaningful work and being appreciated for what I can contribute to the community."

"I like best the job itself. I enjoy working with handicapped children."

"The variety of tasks . . . the sense of doing important things, the good feeling of helping constituents."

## Sharing vs. Part Time

When asked how shared jobs differ from the usual part time work, only a few respondents discuss the social benefits derived from the greater number of jobs produced by the division of full time jobs. Instead, responses center around the fact that restructuring positions has opened jobs which traditionally have been unavailable on a part time basis.

In addition to allowing many partners to continue in their chosen profession at reduced time, job sharing has provided others with an opportunity to begin a new career.

A secretary comments:

". . . it had much value in my particular situation. As an older woman returning to the job market in an area that was not my original career, I feel that I received much good on-the-job training and current experience."

In some cases, the combined talents of the partners fit the requirements of a particular job for which neither partner alone would have qualified.

Many partners perceive a greater "sense of legitimacy" associated with shared jobs than with part time jobs. They feel a greater commitment to their work and to their organization than they would in a part time job. For sharers in many occupations, whether employed or unemployed before partnering, divided jobs give the sense of a whole job. They value:

". . . having a career but not on a full time work schedule."

". . . the fact that commitment to one's job and office is on a more professional level for the job sharer—a career."

### Salary

All respondents have freely chosen to work fewer hours, and many comment that the aspect they like best about job sharing is that the reduced salary is much higher than for the usual part time job. Although many others state that what they like least about job sharing is receiving a half salary, few respondents comment that their salary is not commensurate with the work. It should be remembered, however, that for those who had left their shared jobs, the primary reason was financial.

### Nature of Partnerships

Dividing or partnering provides an alternative access to work and seems to imply, for many respondents, a sense of working at a whole job. Until now, however, partners have been referred to as "sharers," without attempting to assess the accuracy of this term. In order to better understand the advantages and stresses of job sharing, it is necessary to point out the complexity of partner relationships and the difficulty of distinguishing between "shared" and "split" jobs. Generally, "split" jobs have been taken to mean those in which each person is responsible for one-half of the job tasks. "Shared" jobs have been understood to mean that the two partners are together responsible for the total job.

*In practice,* divided jobs cannot be easily categorized by this single dimension. Experiences reported in this study reveal that most positions are not inherently split or separate, i.e., determined basically by the nature of the job alone. Social workers, for example, and others who divide by caseloads, usually do work independently of each other and are perceived as two fractions. "I don't even need to know my other half," is a typical comment. But even among this group, some exhibit a degree of dependency. Other professionals, too, disagree as to whether working independently is a function of the job or of the kind of relationship developed within the partnership. At the other extreme, a rare few positions are wholly collaborative and the totality of tasks is judged as a team accomplishment.

Collaboration does in fact involve specialization—a pattern which may develop as partners work together and learn each other's strengths and weaknesses. Partnerships are not static relationships. Most divided jobs, whether or not they are conceived as such originally, are likely to become cooperative because continuity is to some extent a requisite of most jobs. Indeed, a more thoughtful appraisal would show a spectrum of partner relationships, varying from completely separate to highly collaborative, with the large majority at different points along the scale at different times.

Most of the partners surveyed think their jobs are suitable for sharing because of the variety of skills demanded. More than three times as many respondents feel their partners' skills are complementary to their own rather than the same as their own. Almost 75 percent consider communication essential to working on the job. Moreover, more than half the respondents say that there have been changes in their relationship over time, with most of these indicating movement toward more collaboration rather than toward more separation.

The difficulty of differentiating divided jobs simply as split or shared, separate or collaborative, is significant for two very distinct reasons. First, it suggests that *a priori* division by task analysis *alone* (which has often been the case) is not necessarily the best way for management to envisage restructuring jobs. Second, and more pertinent to this analysis, an appreciation of this complexity is crucial to assessing sharers' perceptions of their sharing relationship and their attitudes toward this as well as other aspects of the divided job.

## MEASURING SHARERS' ATTITUDES ON EFFECTS

Respondents were asked to rate on a five point scale the extent of their agreement or disagreement with statements about the job sharing experience (Table 3-1). As stated above, the data are not appropriate for statistical analysis. However, the respondents' extensive questionnaire and interview comments confirm the patterns suggested by the quantitative survey findings.

Responses to statements about some effects of sharing jobs are clearly more positive than others (see Table 3-1). Ninety-one percent agree that *working fewer hours results in higher energy on the job;* 86 percent agree that their job *allows flexibility in terms of time* and 76 percent agree their job *allows flexibility in terms of task.* But reactions to the statement *sharing enhances your sense of commitment to the organization* were more divided; slightly over half of the respondents agree, a few disagree, and many are undecided. Still fewer agree with the statement that *sharing your job gives you a greater sense of participation in organizational decision-making;* almost a third disagree and slightly more than a third are undecided. Responses to statements about *promotional opportunities* show similar ambivalence; slightly less than half of the respondents agree that their chances were as good as those of full timers in similar positions. Finally, although more than half agree and only 10 percent disagree with the statement *you have a greater opportunity to learn on the job because the work is shared rather than part time,* a large minority (35 percent) is undecided.

The analysis of responses to attitude statements designed to determine the *nature of partner relationships* tends to corroborate the concept of a continuous spectrum rather than separate categories of collaboration and separation. These data, for example, do not match with responses to the item posed earlier in

**Table 3-1**
**Attitudes About Job Sharing: Frequencies**

| | Percentage of respondents | | | | | |
|---|---|---|---|---|---|---|
| | Strongly disagree | Somewhat disagree | Undecided | Somewhat agree | Strongly agree | No. of respondents |
| It was difficult to work out the division of responsibilities between you and your partner. | 73 | 9 | 8 | 8 | 3 | 227 |
| Training in the mechanics of job sharing would have been helpful in the initial design of the position. | 34 | 14 | 31 | 16 | 6 | 222 |
| There is need for close communication between you and your partner. | 6 | 7 | 8 | 15 | 65 | 230 |
| Sharing enhances your sense of responsibility to each other. | 2 | 1 | 19 | 20 | 57 | 232 |
| Sharing enhances your sense of commitment to the organization. | 4 | 7 | 37 | 24 | 28 | 231 |
| Your effectiveness in work is dependent on your partner's performance. | 18 | 16 | 14 | 37 | 15 | 233 |

(continued)

Table 3-1 (continued)

| | Percentage of respondents | | | | | |
| --- | --- | --- | --- | --- | --- | --- |
| | Strongly disagree | Somewhat disagree | Undecided | Somewhat agree | Strongly agree | No. of respondents |
| Successful sharing depends on compatible personalities. | 3 | 6 | 8 | 32 | 52 | 233 |
| Closer collaboration between you and your partner would make job more effective. | 13 | 15 | 37 | 23 | 13 | 226 |
| Working fewer hours results in higher energy on the job. | 1 | 3 | 5 | 16 | 75 | 229 |
| Collaboration enhances the quality of your work, i.e., "two heads are better than one." | 3 | 2 | 11 | 26 | 59 | 232 |
| Sharing your job gives you a greater sense of participation in organizational decision-making. | 11 | 17 | 41 | 14 | 17 | 228 |
| You have a better opportunity to learn on the job because work is shared (rather than part time only). | 4 | 6 | 37 | 25 | 28 | 225 |

| Your job allows flexibility in terms of: | | | | | | |
|---|---|---|---|---|---|
| time | 5 | 4 | 6 | 23 | 63 | 229 |
| task | 7 | 8 | 13 | 34 | 37 | 217 |
| place | 31 | 8 | 28 | 13 | 21 | 204 |
| You have as good a chance of being promoted as: | | | | | | |
| a. a non-sharer (part-time) | 13 | 9 | 33 | 18 | 27 | 184 |
| b. as a full-time person in similar position | 17 | 12 | 22 | 22 | 27 | 192 |
| Your job sharing situation represents a clear model of success. | 3 | 3 | 12 | 24 | 58 | 225 |

the questionnaire: "Do you consider your job split or shared?" Whereas 70 percent of respondents had described their jobs as shared, a higher proportion agree with the statement that *collaboration enhances the quality of your work* and that *successful sharing depends on compatible personalities* (85 percent and 84 percent, respectively). More respondents also agree on the need for *close communication* between partners and that sharing *enhances responsibility* to one's partner (80 percent and 77 percent, respectively). It is interesting, however, that a much smaller number agree that their *effectiveness* depends on partners' performance (52 percent).

## Analysis of Attitude Differences

It is assumed that attitudes of those in partnered jobs would be rooted in the same myriad of reasons underlying any reactions to work, and that the central issues for sharers are no different from those of all workers. But because the question often arises whether sharers are a homogeneous and, therefore, unique population, it is important to determine how much attitudes vary among sharers and to what degree these differences might be applicable to other workers. The evidence of this study suggests that the perception of job sharing advantages does not depend on agreement between partners or on the job level of each individual. It does indicate similarity of reaction based on occupation, longevity on the job, age, type of organization, and, to a lesser degree, team sex composition.

In making these comparisons, individual attitude items which seemed to measure similar attitude dimensions were clustered into seven groups. Clusters were determined by correlating each of the 18 variables with all other variables. The items were clustered as follows:

1. **Mechanics of collaboration:** *(34) It was difficult to work out the division of responsibilities between you and your partner. (35) Training in the mechanics of job sharing would have been helpful in the initial redesign of the position. (41) Closer collaboration between you and your partner would make the job more effective.*

2. **Quality and success:** *(43) Collaboration enhances the quality of your work, i.e., "two heads are better than one." (48) Your job sharing situation represents a clear model of success.*

3. **Closeness or mutual responsibility:** *(36) There is a need for close communication between you and your partner. (37) Sharing enhances your sense of responsibility to each other. (39) Your effectiveness in work is dependent on your partner's performance. (40) Successful sharing depends on compatible personalities.*

4. **Learning on the job:** *(45) You have a better opportunity to learn on the job because the work is shared, rather than part-time only.* This item did not significantly correlate with any other item and does not seem to share in any of the attitude dimensions based on its content.

5. **Organizational commitment:** *(38) Sharing enhances your sense of commitment to the organization. (44) Sharing your job gives you a greater sense of participation in organizational decision-making.*

6. **Promotion:** *(47a) You have as good a chance of being promoted as a non-sharer (part-time). (47b) You have as good a chance of being promoted as a full-time person in a similar position.*

7. **Flexibility:** *(46a, 46b, and 46c) Your job allows flexibility in terms of time, task, place.*

*Within Partnerships*

The difficulty of delineating partner relationships solely by their collaborative or separate nature, already noted in the results to single items, became even more apparent when partner responses were analyzed as teams rather than individuals. In general, for each cluster of statements about job sharing experiences, the partners in about one-third of the teams did not hold the same opinions. Table 3-2 shows the degree of similarity and dissimilarity between partners in a team in their responses to the groups of items about their perceptions and opinions. The area in which there is the most similarity in responses is that of closeness and mutual responsibility. The greatest area of disagreement is that of collaboration. (In answers to the single item regarding the need for time to communicate, there was a great deal of similarity (77 percent) in the answers of partners in a team.)

Table 3-2
Similarity of Perceptions of the Job Sharing Experience Between Partners in a Job Sharing Team

| | Percentage of teams in which partners share similar perceptions | | | Percentage of teams in which partners have |
| | Both agree | Both disagree | Total similarity | different perceptions |
|---|---|---|---|---|
| Closeness or mutual responsibility | 38 | 33 | 71 | 28 |
| Quality and success | 47 | 20 | 67 | 30 |
| Flexibility | 33 | 27 | 60 | 34 |
| Organizational commitment | 29 | 30 | 59 | 37 |
| Learning on the job | 32 | 25 | 57 | 32 |
| Mechanics of collaboration | 29 | 20 | 49 | 48 |
| Promotion | 13 | 26 | 39 | 33 |

*Note:* Percentage summations may not equal 100 because of rounding.

*Job Levels*

No relationship was found between a *person's job level and his/her attitudes on either the effects of sharing or on the partner relationship*. It might be thought that the reaction of those people working in higher or lower levels of authority would vary importantly. Even acknowledging that few respondents are actually low in salary or education (all are high school graduates or above), the importance of this finding should be indicated. It tends to question the assumption that successful job sharing is restricted to individuals in particular levels of education and salary and the inference that only certain jobs, by job definition alone, are suitable for division. Evidence suggests instead that differences are determined by other variables.

## Job Categories

Job categories do show distinctions. In general, teachers and administrators are more likely to show similar attitudes than are sharers in other occupations. For example, they are slightly more than twice as likely as counselors, researchers, and secretaries to agree that closeness is important. (Table 3-3.) They are also twice as likely, as categories, to agree that the quality of their job is enhanced by sharing. (Table 3-4.) Yet researchers as well as administrators are more likely than those in other job categories to believe that their jobs afford them a great deal of *flexibility*. (Table 3-5.)

Distinctions by job category show that administrators and teachers as a group are *less* likely (36 percent and 30 percent, respectively) than counselors, researchers, and secretaries (46 percent, 59 percent, 54 percent) to agree that, as job sharers, they have *opportunities for promotion* similar to those of non-sharers or full time workers. Yet teachers and administrators are somewhat *more likely* than counselors and researchers to believe that job sharing *enhances commitment* to the organization (61 percent and 51 percent for administrators and teachers vs. 33 percent and 39 percent for counselors and researchers). And it is interesting here that the attitudes of secretaries are closer to those of administrators or teachers (with 45 percent agreeing that job sharing increases commitment).

**Table 3-3**
**Attitude Cluster: Closeness or Mutual Responsibility**

| | Percentage of sharers in each occupational category who agree or disagree | |
|---|---|---|
| | Agree | Disagree |
| Administrator | 65 | 35 |
| Teacher | 71 | 29 |
| Counselor | 29 | 71 |
| Researcher | 26 | 74 |
| Secretary | 31 | 69 |
| Other | 55 | 45 |

**Table 3-4**
**Attitude Cluster: Quality and Success**

| | Percentage of sharers in each occupational category who agree or disagree | |
|---|---|---|
| | Agree | Disagree |
| Administrator | 75 | 26 |
| Teacher | 80 | 20 |
| Counselor | 48 | 52 |
| Researcher | 47 | 53 |
| Secretary | 44 | 56 |
| Other | 56 | 44 |

*Note:* Percentage summations may not equal 100 because of rounding.

**Table 3-5**
**Attitude Cluster: Flexibility**

| | Percentage of sharers in each occupational category who agree or disagree | |
|---|---|---|
| | Agree | Disagree |
| Administrator | 78 | 22 |
| Teacher | 46 | 54 |
| Counselor | 52 | 48 |
| Researcher | 63 | 37 |
| Secretary | 32 | 68 |
| Other | 40 | 60 |

*Age*

There are several other factors which relate to occupational variations. Age differences appear to affect attitudes. People in their twenties are less likely to agree that job sharing enhances their *commitment to the organization,* that the oldest sharers (51-64) are much *less* likely to agree that job sharing increases the flexibility of their job. (Tables 3-6 and 3-7.) Yet people in the same age group (51-64) are somewhat more inclined to feel a greater *opportunity to learn* on the job. Those in their forties are more likely than those in their twenties to believe that job sharing contributes to the quality of their work. (Table 3-8.)

**Table 3-6**
**Attitude Cluster: Organizational Commitment**

|  | Percentage of sharers in each age group who agree or disagree | |
|---|---|---|
|  | Agree | Disagree |
| 21 - 30 | 35 | 65 |
| 31 - 40 | 56 | 44 |
| 41 - 50 | 44 | 56 |
| 51 - 64 | 56 | 44 |

**Table 3-7**
**Attitude Cluster: Flexibility**

|  | Percentage of sharers in each age group who agree or disagree | |
|---|---|---|
|  | Agree | Disagree |
| 21 - 30 | 40 | 60 |
| 31 - 40 | 64 | 37 |
| 41 - 50 | 57 | 43 |
| 51 - 64 | 25 | 75 |

*Note:* Percentage summations may not equal 100 because of rounding.

**Table 3-8**
**Attitude Cluster: Quality and Success**

|  | Percentage of sharers in each age group who agree or disagree | |
|---|---|---|
|  | Agree | Disagree |
| 21 - 30 | 43 | 57 |
| 31 - 40 | 68 | 32 |
| 41 - 50 | 76 | 24 |
| 51 - 64 | 65 | 35 |

### Length of Time on Job

These age distinctions, however should not be confused with the length of time on the job. Individuals who have been working in divided jobs for *less than a year* are more likely to feel they have an *opportunity to learn* than those in such jobs for a longer period of time. Yet those who have been *longer in the job* are somewhat more likely to feel more *flexibility* than are recent sharers.

### Type of Organization

The type of organization and type of schedule also bear on attitudes. Individuals tend to agree more on the need for closeness when they are employed in either private organizations, whether nonprofit or profit, or in public education, and least when employed in government. (Table 3-9.) More specifically, those partners employed in private nonprofit organizations and public education are most likely to agree that quality is enhanced by sharing. (Table 3-10.) Furthermore, sharers whose work time is arranged in split weeks (as well as all overlapping time) are most likely to agree that closeness is more important than those in other schedules, such as half days. (Table 3-11.)

### Sex

Differences in types of teams are worth noting. Respondents in male/female teams are *less* likely than those in female/female teams to agree that job sharing *enhanced the quality and success*

**Table 3-9**
**Attitude Cluster: Closeness or Mutual Responsibility**

| | Percentage of sharers in different types of organizations who agree or disagree | |
|---|---|---|
| | Agree | Disagree |
| Private nonprofit | 59 | 41 |
| Private profit | 53 | 47 |
| Government | 30 | 70 |
| Public education | 65 | 35 |

**Table 3-10**
**Attitude Cluster: Quality and Success**

| | Percentage of sharers in different types of organizations who agree or disagree | |
|---|---|---|
| | Agree | Disagree |
| Private nonprofit | 62 | 38 |
| Private profit | 58 | 42 |
| Government | 51 | 49 |
| Public education | 73 | 27 |

**Table 3-11**
**Attitude Cluster: Closeness or Mutual Responsibility**

| | Percentage of sharers in different time schedules who agree or disagree | |
|---|---|---|
| | Agree | Disagree |
| Half days | 47 | 53 |
| Split weeks | 60 | 40 |
| Week on-off | 44 | 56 |
| All time overlap | 71 | 29 |
| Not fixed | 36 | 65 |
| Other | 22 | 78 |

*of their work* (50 percent, 68 percent, respectively). Respondents in the very small category of male/male teams were less likely to agree with statements related to quality of work than those in either of the other two combinations. They were also less likely to agree with statements regarding closeness, organizational commitment, opportunities for promotion, and flexibility.

## PRINCIPAL ISSUES

### REWARDS

#### Shorter Hours and Time and Task Trading

Job sharers value working fewer hours; respondents state that work is better accomplished because tedious jobs are less so and stressful work is less draining. Clerical workers are more inclined than others to offer time off as most rewarding. One comments:

> "The best part is working week on, week off. Once you have learned the Mag II machine, the work is routine and boring for the most part, because it is straight typing all day."

A social worker says:

> "What I like best is that I'm not always being tired, but able to come back to work refreshed rather than always being under pressure."

From many occupations, partners write that they have time for such things as attending night meetings or preparing for the next day of work. But respondents perceive time at work as better not only because of shorter hours, but also because it is flexible within the total required hours.

Whether partners work in collaboration or separately, the presence of another person or "half" with whom to trade time brings satisfaction. This flexibility is dependent on partner relationships as well as the job requirements per se. For example, all social and probation workers and many counselors have separate caseloads. Many do not know each other, yet a few trade time. "We can occasionally cover for each other in crisis situations," writes a probation officer, "and have come to know each other well enough so that we could implement a continuous service to clients even though we are not usually involved with all of them." Among those other professionals who perceive their work as essentially "split" there is also a time tradeoff. A city planner who divides his work by separate responsibilities writes:

"We often switch days when it suits our separate work loads. Other tasks, where no one seems to care, we can give to the other, but one is still responsible."

Teachers and administrators, on the other hand, who tend to work more closely, often cite the advantage of partner flexibility. A common statement is:

"What I like best is the flexibility built into our job. In an emergency one partner can cover for the other."

Others report:

"We fill in for each other if something special comes up. We can trade days as long as we check with out employer." (clerk)

"If either I or my partner needed a full day off, the other would work the entire day. Employer did not object as long as one of us was on the job to accomplish the work." (secretary)

"The job is incredibly boring and because my partner is cooperative and flexible, it is easier to take time off." (receptionist)

"It is flexible time because we do not have to work the same days every week, we just decide who wants to work when." (medical technician)

"We are happier employees because we switch time and hours without involving our employer. We switch without money exchange, but with the owing and repaying of hours between the two of us. We are able to cover for each other at any time and feel free to do so." (secretary)

Partnerships allow for even more supportive tradeoffs because teaming often permits each individual to choose tasks by preference and/or competence. In this way, a tedious or pressured job becomes more bearable because each partner can concentrate on a limited area, which affords a greater sense of effectiveness and confidence.

### Dimensions of Partner Support

The opportunity to use a partner as a continuous "sounding board" adds another dimension to the feeling of support: a sense of learning and a relief from total responsibility. "Partners bolster each other to dare to do things that one might not attempt alone," writes a school resource director, "and if in doubt, one can consult the other and prevent mistakes." "You have less pressure," says a researcher, "and the feeling of having another resource and source of wisdom when you feel yourself at wit's end." The sense of interdependence is expressed in varying phrases.

Many are grateful for the opportunity to share responsibility for the whole job. "Decision making can be a lonely process," or "the job is challenging but the whole job doesn't rest on my shoulders alone," are typical comments. "Sharing means having help making difficult, complex decisions, someone who is as interested as I am in finding ideas for solution."

Even in the jobs which would not apparently elicit these reactions, support has other dimensions. A laboratory technician writes, "I felt much more comfortable sharing a job—more interested in the ramifications of my work and less bogged down by the many details that need attention given the nature of the job." A clerical worker reiterates this thought: "There's an added self-awareness, more of a focus on your job since you and your partner communicate more often while the rest of the office ignore you and your job. You don't feel so neglected or ignored." For many sharers, partnering gives a sense of belonging: "I felt more of a part of the whole than an isolated fraction," writes an administrative officer.

## A Sense of Effectiveness

Partners feel better able to perform the work, many jobs, more thoroughly and effectively. The result for many partners is a sense of competency and added esteem. "We have the opportunity to run several small groups at a time and get to know the children more effectively," writes a teacher. "Sharing means problems and solutions" another adds, "and learning new methods and techniques of instruction." "I can be better prepared," writes another.

"This is different," writes a secretary, "because of feedback from partner, a reality check to catch mistakes and correct them." Another respondent comments, "Two people are able to be in two places at one time." For several partners, as an administrator writes: "The energy of two sources means that a balance may ultimately be better struck which is much more stable than on one individual's energy alone."

## PROBLEMS

### Time

Time and partnership rewards, however, must be weighed against the stresses they also carry. How to limit one's time can become a matter of real concern. For a medical intern, sharing still means dividing a full time job of 80-100 hours a week. "Therefore, it is more accurate to say that we are sharing a double time job—each of us averages 40 hours a week all year."

Even when tasks are clearly delineated, the nature of many jobs is such that work extends to non-work time. A social worker writes that "the emotional stress of the job carries over to off time and emergencies oftentimes have to be handled then." Another adds: "In order to make myself available to clients I do offer my home phone number and thus I do receive a great many calls at home. However, this is more than compensated for by the privilege of working part time."

In only a few instances do sharers attribute time pressure to particular schedules, though it should be noted that working half days for some respondents defeats shorter hours because of commuting or "gearing up" for work. Overtime is rarely perceived as an expectation of the supervisor. Respondents are much more likely to acknowledge their own sense of commitment to the work and to the job itself as a major reason for feeling stress. Even with a partner, they report that it is often hard to accomplish as much as they would like. Teachers are not alone in reporting: "The job feels almost like a full time job with a lot more flexibility . . . ;" or "sometimes I feel like I'm doing five days work in two and one-half days." Sharers, including some whose jobs would appear more limited, comment:

"I tend to spend too much time on the job."

"An enormous amount of work must be taken home. There's never enough time."

"There's a frustration of never being there quite enough to feel like everything is done thoroughly."

"It's hard to squeeze everything that needs doing into three workdays. I do work some overtime and take things home to read, think, and write about."

"It's hard to control hours and tasks and too easy to allow yourself to put in extra hours. It's hard to keep a creative job to half time!"

"I make myself available for evening meetings, willing to fill in when needed. If I were only working part time, I would not feel the need to go beyond 'the call of duty,' i.e., those hours I am hired to work in."

Married partners especially find it difficult to turn work on and off. "There's never enough time to play," write both husband and wife. A wife sharing with her husband reports that not only is it difficult to adjust because "the initial moments/hours of the day are a jolt . . . and when I'm finished, I can't always switch gears successfully. There is a tendency to work overtime and make the job the center of our married relationship."

*Being Special*

For many partners the sense of commitment to one's partner and to the organization is heightened because sharers perceive themselves as examples of a new way to work. This self-consciousness becomes both a challenge and potential problem.

"Our situation is an unqualified success, I believe, because we both want to work part time so much that we try extra hard to make things run smoothly . . . . Also, we were the city employees to be allowed to try the experiment and we were not about to let it fail. (We both have much more enthusiasm for our jobs than the full time library staff.)"

"The supervisor as well as partners are trying hard to make the position successful. We are trial cases in our organization so the future of job sharing depends on us somewhat."

"Since we are the first, we were eager to make the program work. Therefore, we are careful to do our job and not 'goof off.' We are happy with our situation and it reflects on our performance. Some staff feared our 'split' would result in additional work for them but this has not happened."

". . . productivity is greater, but in a way this is a disadvantage to the job sharer because he ends up working far and beyond what a normal worker does to keep up the employer's confidence in job sharing."

"There is a tendency to work more than the specified hours (in a salaried position) to be sure you're putting in enough work; a tendency to want to make job sharing work well so more departments will try it."

*Personal Partner Adjustments*

Partnership is basically a work relationship. Although many sharers report knowing each other prior to being employed together, most do not share outside social activities. Most partners do, however, need to cooperate in coordinating daily details, or in more complex planning and problem solving, and especially when it becomes crucial to eliminate possible team inconsistencies in dealing with others. Compatibility, flexibility, "going the extra mile," and above all, *trust*, are the expressions partners repeat constantly. Respondents' statements often refer to the need for maturity and intelligence vs. irresponsibility, inability to criticize constructively, being overly competitive, and defensiveness. Only a few sharers, however, indicate such problems as incompatible traits or incompetency.

The need to care about and be sensitive to the person sharing the position does involve adjustments. As one writes:

> "Having to think about the other person in the way that one does adds a unique dimension. (Very pleasant and constructive when it works, disastrous, I should think, if there are personality or logistical problems.)"

Some partnership problems are exacerbated by strong personality differences; others are perhaps inherent in sharing. A teacher writes:

> "It's sometimes frustrating to start a project/unit with kids and have my partner finish or to finish a unit which she started and which I'm not particularly excited or comfortable with."

One respondent notes that "the ego connection with the job must be foregone" in the job sharing context. Some regret the loss of personal recognition. A planner writes:

> "I am very good at analysis and writing and my partner was very effective in dealing with people. It seemed an optimal use of our talents for her to present the work I had done—but then I resented not getting credit in public when, in fact, I had done all the work."

A librarian explains her dislike of the "loss of complete responsibility and partial loss of identity." An assistant planning director comments on missing a sense of personal reward, "having to share compliments on work done." Even in a satisfying personal relationship, she feels that "some work should be done individually to maintain self-confidence." In another instance, a secretary notes:

> "It was apparent from the start that we were opposites (e.g., a generation apart in age; years apart in education) with wide discrepancies in job attitude and aims. I needed areas of responsibility for which I was solely accountable. I suspect my partner did, too."

Many sharers point to the need for lack of possessiveness about work and to the difficulties encountered when one or another has a strong sense of ownership. "People tend to keep 'their' work to their desk," writes a clerical worker. Another comments:

> "Most executive secretaries do not want to share their responsibilities because there would be a certain 'giving up' of power. They protect their bosses and there is usually some kind of personality bond between the two."

A program director explains in more positive terms:

> "In my experience, my sense of responsibility for the total program has increased, while my sense of ownership for my individual piece has decreased. I feel a sense of shared responsibility for and pride in work of others when all I have done is react to it."

## Adjustments Within the Organization

Many partners are especially sensitive about the need to maintain contact with full time staff. The usual socializing is more difficult because of working half time. Some respondents agree with the partner who says:

> "There seems to be a bit of jealousy from other staff members from time to time—of our freedom to come and go. We have to remind people that we only get half salary. They seem to forget that."

In other instances difficulties have occurred when a divided position is initiated without adequate explanation to other staff. Since partnerships are rare in the organization, as a sharer reports, there is a lack of understanding that "we are two equals instead of one boss and one employee; the result often is not being informed of meetings and memos."

Problems of continuity may be aggravated by poor communication. But some respondents still find that, whatever the reason, being on the job only half time makes it difficult to "keep up with what is happening with other staff." Many partners stress the importance of extra efforts to communicate with ancillary staff. Although this is often mitigated by one partner informing the other, it necessitates that sharers be especially well organized.

Even then, however, a loosely structured organization can complicate partnership adjustments. One respondent described scheduling difficulties that result from such things as last minute changes in meeting times. Disorganized settings frustrate the successful team functioning for at least a few partners. Although many sharers like best the opportunity to work independently as teams with minimum supervision and are gratified by a sense of responsibility, others seek authority and dislike a lack of direction and supervision. Some ask for more clear-cut job definitions. What is likely to happen in these instances is that sharers may tend to lean more on each other:

> "We find the job challenging and stimulating on a personal level. Organizationally we find it somewhat frustrating as we were just put here and our knowledge has been acquired the hard way. The fact that we were partners helped us to work on this together. Either one of us alone might have given up."

A few partners feel that they are still seen within the organization as less professional than full time workers. This often appears more related to fears about an uncertain future than to the immediate circumstances.

WHO BENEFITS?

*Value to Organization*

Respondents feel strongly that the organization benefits from partnerships as much as they, and that job sharing should not be viewed merely as a privilege.

". . . sharers have energy, enthusiasm and loyalty to the job. It is more of a symbiotic relationship because organization and employee needs are met simultaneously."

"I'm convinced by my own experience that the agency gets more input and better quality work from split code teams than from the average worker."

"If organizations knew how much more work they could get out of two part timers than one full time, I think they would be surprised."

They point out that there is better coverage with two individuals on the job:

"When special projects require extra or overtime work, we are generally able to work full time. I think this provides the organization with an ideal situation. There is someone to do the extra work who does not need to be trained; we can also cover for one another when one of us is ill."

"For our office there is the availability at all times of at least one member of our office. The organization can call upon us for emergency or temporary jobs. If one of us should choose to leave, it does not have to train a new person while still maintaining efficient flow in the office."

Many speak of covering for each other when one is ill. Teachers especially note that substitutes need not be called in. In stressful jobs, some report as this social worker:

"Allowing workers to go part time allows them to continue work whereas before due to emotional strain, workers oftentimes were forced to quit. With fewer burn-outs there are fewer positions that have to be filled by people needing training."

Public contact jobs are better filled by sharers, partners feel, "because of the additional energy which helps one deal with the public in a pleasant way." A consumer complaint coordinator says: "One can't maintain a sensitivity in this job eight hours a day."

Efficiency on the job becomes an advantage not only because of greater energy but from "lower error rate due to checking each other's work," as a clerical worker claims; or "because of an absolute necessity to organize well and record all procedures," as a librarian writes.

## Job Insecurity

Many sharers feel that, while they are at least as effective and often more so than their full time counterparts, they are not accorded equal treatment in terms of promotion and job tenure.

Many jobs are designed as temporary, some because they are part of short term experiments. In at least one instance, the experiment is designed so that only the "original" partner remains beyond the time period and, as one writes:

". . . even if the new partner is job sharing as part of an experiment, she should *care* about the job if only not to 'wreck the system' for the permanent partner."

Even where the organization has established policy, each case is still decided on an individual basis, and the uncertainty of renewal concerns many partners. A librarian in a community college writes that, although the shared job has worked well for six years,

"and our work is given high marks by our director, it has been a battle every year except the last to be given the right to carry on as sharers. We still have no tenure or certainty that we will be permitted to go on. I have resisted pressure for years to go full time."

A teacher worries that:

"After five years of half time work I am still the first to go if school enrollment drops."

The impossibility of advancement poses a very real problem to others. County workers explain:

"There is no chance of promotion for part time employees in clerical positions. Civil Service rules make it difficult to change job specs."

"To be promoted to a supervisory level a person must return to full time status."

For others the slower progress on the salary scale and slower rate of seniority is a decided disadvantage. Some teachers are frustrated by the inability to accumulate time toward tenure, at any rate as long as they work half time. Teachers, too, seem to be most concerned about "being placed in limbo" in returning to a full time contract. Some systems (teaching or civil service) have expressly mandated rules for reverting to full time, others have left the question open.

RESPONDENTS' VIEWS ON THE
FUTURE EXPANSION OF JOB SHARING

Respondents have a personal stake in the extension of partnered jobs. Conscious of "being different," they feel the need for other examples, for recognition within the organization and in the larger work world. "Make good jobs available—not just at lower levels" is a common plea. Good jobs are those which include prorated salaries and prorated benefits, at all occupational levels. Half salaries at *low level jobs only,* respondents assert, will not allow a sufficient number of potential partners and provide the continuity for the organization or for the individual worker.

*Obstacles*

Sharers are well aware, however, of the obstacles in creating additional job sharing arrangements. The major obstacle they foresee, elaborated on throughout this study, is the lack of legitimacy accorded to part time work. Although they themselves consider that work can be effectively performed on a less than full time basis, they clearly recognize that society does not. This is especially true for partners in professions. The few men who are sharing are especially sensitive:

"You make less money, work fewer hours and are then considered unambitious, uninterested in career . . . odd and probably un-American to boot!"

Another young man feels that co-workers, "trapped in their expensive type of life-styles," resent others' freedom of choice and perceive all those who work fewer hours as less serious.

Most partners also point to the general lack of awareness of job sharing. Many comment that other workers are surprised to hear of their arrangements. Even in a county office where splitting jobs has been a practice for several years, a partner writes, "I had never heard of it before we started." At this time, only a few organizations who employ sharers advertise, for fear of unmanageable numbers of applicants. Knowledge of current experience is limited, if not nil.

The general resistance to change, even where sharing has occurred, is acknowledged as a real barrier.

"Any change in a sacred institution such as the working structure will be viewed as a threat. There are real and imagined fears . . . ."

Another writes, that "it doesn't *have to be,* but it does sound complicated, time consuming, etc., to an employer."

Sharers also recognize the organizational complications. A few indicate that administrators naturally favor those jobs which are apparently more easily divisible. They admit that supervisors find difficulty in envisaging the sharing of authority. One writes:

"We have found the creation of part time positions much more workable, flexible and acceptable to higher management. Administration requires responsibility and accountability for work to be done—and sharing a position blurs these lines . . . ."

This is reiterated by a respondent who feels that the concept of sharing is a "concession that work naturally breaks down into 40-hour modules." She notes that although in some cases sharing will naturally evolve, "there is more to be gained from pushing career part time options and de-emphasizing the sharing aspects."

In contrast, many others incline to the view that administrative and managerial positions "seem to lend themselves to sharing because of added responsibility and decision making." An organizational developer comments:

> "I have heard it argued that there are jobs/positions which would be inappropriate for sharing. I don't feel that way. I am convinced that any job can be shared . . . ."

He adds, however, that organizational support and personal desire for success are necessary.

*Needs*

Organizational support is as important as sharers' competency in respondents' discussion of the requirements for success of all partnered jobs. Most concur with the observation that:

> "An organization that gives only lip service to the idea, or worse yet, an administration that didn't like it could make a partnership difficult."

Many comments refer to the importance of having management that is open to and supportive of the idea of job sharing, and fellow employees who are flexible enough to accommodate to change.

Whatever the nature of the partnership, respondents are inclined to write of the need for clearly defined total job responsibilities. Sharers in administrative positions are more likely than others to say that work should be well defined, but many others, as indicated in earlier pages, ask for clarification of job limits. Respondents are concerned too that there be an understanding from superiors that individuals within partnerships have "boundaries so that responsibility and accountability come into play."

There is less agreement as to who should have the authority to define the job limits. One disgruntled respondent writes "the organization should not abdicate its responsibility to control the relationship between sharers." In more separate partnerships, sharers often write of the satisfaction "of having control to do one's own work" or of "being able to work independently of partner." In more collaborative relationships we often hear: "We are successful because we have freedom with minimal supervision;" or "Our supervisor was willing to let us work things out the best way for ourselves."

In all divided jobs, there is less agreement about who should be allowed to share. The matching of partners, obviously, is of varying importance, depending on the way the position is perceived by the organization and by the sharers. Although some respondents emphasize the need for partners experienced in the organization, others complain that seniority rules restrict other qualified applicants within the organization. Certain respondents in more collaborative partnerships ask for "consultation" with the incumbent when a new half is to be hired.

Sharers wish to see the extension of restructured jobs and yet are well aware of the difficulties for both workers and institutions. As elaborated in chapter one, the policy initiatives for many flexible work schemes are of recent origin. Future examination of the issues will focus on the advantages and complications for the organization. At this time, job sharing, in particular, has involved such small numbers that its value can best be described within each work setting and with particular individuals.

The following chapter presents selected profiles of sharers and their supervisors.

# Chapter Four

# Partnership Profiles

This chapter is the result of hundreds of hours of conversations with 84 individuals—job sharers, their supervisors, and many of their co-workers.[1] It illustrates, in their own words, the feelings of success or of disappointment with job sharing. Comments reveal the outcome, in each instance, of the special combination of attributes and attitudes of partners, receptivity of other staff, and requisites of the particular job tasks.

Partnerships which encompass a variety of occupations, levels, and types of sharing arrangements have been selected. The groupings within these sections are arbitrary. They reflect the author's judgment of a certain commonality of many aspects, and might have been categorized differently. Taken as a whole, however, the partnership profiles reveal most clearly the reasons individuals have wanted to work as partners and the ways in which they, as individuals and as teams, have developed relationships within the spectrum of cooperation. Some positions have been included which are considered separate, but the emphasis is on those which are collaborative, particularly because they might have seemed less amenable to joint responsibility.

The profiles are presented in a further attempt to address the question of whether sharers are a unique population in special

---

1. Some partners were interviewed individually, others jointly, as circumstances permitted.

jobs, or if, instead, they provide models for a larger segment of the labor force who may wish to balance their work life patterns by venturing the choice of job sharing.

SPLIT OR SHARED?

*Medical Clerks: Cooperation for Continuity*

*Ann and Barbara, medical clerks in a county office, officially "split a code." Their position, however, has become more than a combination of two part time jobs, since responsibility for the total job is actually shared. Each partner works specific days and performs all necessary tasks, but certain parts which are more suited to the skills of one person are assumed by that partner. Their supervisor recognized the team's efficiency. "The key thing," she points out, "is continuity, so nothing gets lost in the day-to-day routine."*

"I worked the job alone for eight months before we split it," Ann explains. "I don't see myself lasting more than a year and a half if we hadn't, because I get bored in this kind of job. Right now I want to work part time—not so much for the money, but just to keep my sanity. I have only one child and he's only seven. Maybe by the time I'm 30 or 35 I could afford, emotionally, to spend less time at home and more time worrying about a job." Ann also wanted time to go back to school and earn an associate degree.

Her partner, Barbara, in her mid-forties and the mother of five teenagers, had worked elsewhere in the same office. "My husband was furious when I first went back to work, but he has finally come to accept the fact that I could be a total dud if I didn't work. It's helped financially as well. My husband has had a couple of rather serious illnesses that my benefits have paid for. Plus the dental insurance—we have three kids in orthodontics."

Although the county system has since formalized the procedure for splitting jobs, the fact that both women had worked in the same office made the changeover relatively simple at the time. Both were known to their supervisor, who had arranged a similar split position earlier.

Tracking the process through each level of administration and personnel was hard, the supervisor explains, ". . . but so many things are achievable if you can just strategize what you're going to end up doing and point out the benefits. I certainly wasn't aware that this was a new approach to employment." In this instance, she commented, she had two capable, well qualified people, one of whom could train the other, and the change meant that a full time position would be made available for another hire.

"We decided to work specific days," Barbara says, "so that Ann could have her time off to go to school. I'd never wanted to do half days; once you get your body out of the house you might as well work." Basically, they do the same tasks; each works at computing, transcribing, writing reports, ordering materials and covering the phone. But from the beginning, both partners realized a sense of dependency on each other.

"Barbara has worked in the system many more years than I have," explains Ann, "so she knows her way around. That helped me—plus her good will came with her when she came to this job. It's hard working in a place this big if you aren't known, and I sort of found that a big hump to get over when I first started working here. As far as working together in a real collaboration," she remarks, "we don't do that. But oftentimes I'll start something and ask if she can improve it or the other way around. To a certain extent we divide some things, mainly for continuity. We depend mostly on notes."

They also divide by interest and expertise. "Ann is a math genius, where I'm a real dud," Barbara says. "She's got a quick mind regarding budgeting things—like invoices and accounting—so she's done that." Barbara herself prefers writing reports and is beginning to learn from her partner's experience in the budgeting. Each feels that she is judged individually, but each still relies on her partner to cover when needed. "I don't mind if Ann is sick or something . . . . I'm happy to come in and take over." They take some responsibility for working out vacation schedules together with their supervisor.

The supervisor explains that she does look to each for different tasks, but sees them doing more as a team and expanding the job. "They are a great combination, and do learn from each other. They're sometimes more like consultants than typists, and we get a lot of extra work done. They come in each day motivated and motivate each other. I don't have to spend my supervisory time worrying about that."

"This particular pair," she reiterates, "is certainly more productive than many individuals who work full time. Many people sort of settle into a job, they learn what they can do or avoid doing, and don't bring the same kind of renewed spirit when they come in daily."

Both partners speak of how their shared job differs from part time work. "Part time sounds to me," says Barbara, "like there's not enough work for a full time person and the job is in a smaller time frame . . . it's all yours. Now, job sharing is a whole different focus. If two people like each other, it's an opportunity to help each other, which is always pleasurable. I think you have to feel comfortable with the person you're sharing with and I don't think its a 50-50 proposition. It's more like 60-70 or 80-80. I think each partner has to make an effort."

"It's worked out even better than I thought," Ann adds. "Certainly better than part time, because I would have been doing 40 hours worth of work trying to get it all done." She had worried about being expected to work beyond the allotted hours, "especially because I had been in it full time and knew how much work there was. But Barbara is not the type to let it happen. And the supervisor is always careful to see that everything is all right. I don't think other staff resent our half time; after all, we make less salary. Our supervisor is so flexible because she's the type of person who wants you to be happy in your job. And that's really important for everyone here. But part time just would not get the job done . . . because it's a full time job."

"This has given me a chance to learn and to grow," Barbara reflects, "and to interact with people. But then, on the other hand, it's given me the opportunity to do the woman things which I enjoy and feel that I should do. You know, having been brainwashed by the *Ladies Home Journal* in my teenage years—we were all going to be able to take our little secretarial jobs, meet Mr. Right, get married and then have children and live happily ever after. So said the *Ladies Home Journal.* I had never been to college, other than a year after high school. I'm a college dropout this quarter because of feeling pushed, but I will go back again. Anyway, I think that working part time and sharing a job gives me the best of both worlds.''

## Physicians: Professional and Domestic Responsibilities

*Two female physicians, who have been working together for the past three years, share child care responsibilities as well as professional ones. The sharing of a position in order for partners to relieve each other with child care might appear more usual with married couples, a situation described in later profiles. The following example might appear to be a singular model because it is within a highly professional position. However, many sharing instances exist for similar reasons in England, where certain banks have instituted a system of "twinning." These arrangements, for clerical workers particularly, provide alternating weekly schedules for pairs of women, sometimes in the same job. "Twins" care for each other's children as well as their own during periods when they are not on the job. Utilizing such auxiliary staff, the banks maintain, allows them to retain experienced personnel.*

In this partnership, the sense of being a team doesn't come from the nature of the position, which is essentially split, but from being allowed to maintain their professional status.

After the birth of her first child, Ruth might have continued to practice on a part time basis, but explains, "I had the problem of what would I do about the baby sitting. And Martha would have had the same problem. So, why not just become one person and alternate the baby sitting and the working?''

Martha adds, "I think anybody could job share in some fields of medicine any time. A much bigger problem would be to find someone whom you would enjoy sharing with or finding someone who would have a reason. Without the baby care, I would have had no reason.''

The logistics of working together within the regulations of the hospital were complicated. Ruth, who had been full time, asked to split the load with Martha, who was not working on the staff at that time. The department head was willing because he had been trying desperately to get additional help. "I was glad for help showing up in any form," he explains. However, Ruth was already on the way to becoming a partner in the group practice and needed to work more than half time to retain that status. Now, having reached partnership status, she continues to work more than half time and her partner less than half time. There are, then, significant penalties for Martha, who is officially considered "part time temporary" and receives no fringe benefits.

Apparently, the financial inequity is more than outweighed by the flexibility the arrangement affords them.

Martha credits the supervisor for his understanding support in initiating the team. "If I had not had children and had come here for a full time job, I don't think I would feel as committed as I do now. They took a risk and they have been highly understanding about maternity leave and things like that. They have dealt very fairly with me and my problems and it makes me feel a strong commitment that I don't think would have been there otherwise. If I had come here full time to make some money only, I would have been, in a way, more judgmental about the whole thing."

Individual patient care is not really shared. Ruth does feel greater confidence in the sharing relationship, however. "There is on-going contact," she says, "even when I'm not physically here. I feel that I have someone who is committed to my patients. If I only worked, say three days a week, sure I could say to someone else in the department: 'Hey, would you see my post-ops tomorrow?' but I wouldn't feel that that person had the same commitment to my patients.''

Martha, who is more inclined to describe the arrangement as "split," explains the working of the group service: "If I have a reason for a patient to be seen the next day, usually between us all patients get seen. But, if for a particular reason, there's a problem, I just tell Ruth about it and ask her to check. To that extent, there's a little bit of sharing, but no more than there would be if she wasn't working the next day. I would just ask someone else to do it. We all cooperate among ourselves that way.''

The extra relationship does mean, however, that they can arrange to cover for each other if one of their own children is ill; or if one is working late and on call, the other will take over domestic chores. "She'll feed dinner to my children," says Martha, "or, if I get no dinner, I can come to her place until my husband gets home."

While the nature of the work is split, both feel a sense of sharing. "You do need two people," comments Ruth, "who are very well able to work together. You have to want it very much, consider it a very important thing to do, and work into it." Each considers it essential to her success that their knowledge of medicine is pretty much on a par. Martha says, "I think that if I felt Ruth was not as good as I was, or vice-versa, it would be difficult. You could manage that in a co-worker, but not in a sharer."

Trust and support in the other gives both a sense of greater involvement with the hospital. "I know what's happening the three days I'm not there," Martha notes. "I get all the gossip from Ruth—and I mean the good gossip. And she hears what's going on the days she isn't there. It's important. You don't feel like you're the stranger. You hear the personal stuff and the medical things. We see each other every day when we pick up and drop off the kids. It's almost a little ritual. You have a cup of tea ready, sit down and talk about any problems."

Although their supervisor sees them as two distinct personalities, he appreciates this sense of teamwork. "This is their particular thing," he says, "that they share how many times they turn around in a day. There is practically absolute communication between them. And you can assume that on a given day one knows everything the other one did the previous day or what anybody else did. I can't think that all people would share that freely."

Being perceived as a team is important to both women. "We've tried very hard not to upset them," Ruth explains, "and to make sure that we really work as one person."

Although their medical specialty is one where demand exceeds supply, part time positions are often seen as stepping stones to private practice. For this reason, they sometimes feel they are viewed suspiciously by other hospital staff.

"There is only one classification of a part time person," admits their supervisor. "And this is the person you bring in for a week to get the job done. I cannot sell the idea that there are part time people committed on a lifetime basis, thoroughly committed to the organization and doing a tremendous job in terms of helping us improve our quality of care and really putting a lot of work into it."

Professional resistance concerns both Ruth and Martha. "There is a very strong element of feeling that part time people are somehow not as devoted," Ruth asserts. "And I think people make decisions based on that feeling, sort of an emotional reaction, rather than on the facts. They make it almost impossible for you to raise your family and do it (practice medicine) and then they turn around and say, 'see what a terrible job you're doing.' "

But neither woman is ready yet to consider a full time position, even though, as Martha notes, each admits to misgivings about ". . . putting our careers on the back burner. Promotion is something you really can't consider when working part time."

Ruth had originally planned to work full time later on when all her children were in school. "But now that I see how much time child care takes," she comments, "I think they almost need you more then. There's so much going on."

Martha, who considers teaching a future possibility, is grateful that, for the time being, she can continue to stay in medicine through this arrangement, however inequitable financially. "Part of me," she explains, "says, 'I don't care' (about benefits). If you compare me to other physicians, some of them are working more and making, per hour, a lot less. Compared to jobs that most people have, I have a lot more. Even working half time I make a tiny bit less than my husband does."

Both she and her husband grew up understanding the insecurity of unemployment. "We just like the idea of knowing that the wolves will not be at the door. We both have life insurance and all of that, but this is better than any life insurance."

*Media Specialists: Part Time Alone, Part Time Together*

*Laura and Evelyn have worked together for four years as reading resource teachers in a school district where the administration has not encouraged either part time or sharing. These women chose pairing originally as a way to stay part time when the district received funding to make each of their jobs full time at two different schools. Both have children, Evelyn three teenagers and Laura two younger. Selecting the school where Laura was already working, they found that the principal and the personnel officer were shifting their own jobs and were not concerned about "setting precedent." The women had carefully organized a joint position in which they serve as consultants to teachers and parents—ordering texts, administering tests, working out problems with students and parents, and writing original curriculum materials.*

*Their current principal calls them "two of the finest I've worked with who strive to provide program continuity. Although their half time contracts don't imply another half, these two make sure to communicate. They share in terms of their extra or volunteer responsibilities."*

The work lends itself both to division and to collaboration. Since each woman had already worked with different grade levels, as a pair they could continue similar patterns and arbitrarily divide special events. They were careful, at the beginning, to maintain a sense of equal time as far as possible.

"We do so much coordinating and organizing generally," Laura explains, "in a sense like middle managers dealing with people, not a product. A resource job is really a lot of junk, where you become a natural sounding block for problems." The principal is busy and in a judgmental position. "We, on the other hand, don't have a lot of clout, but can listen and be supportive." She acknowledges, however, that theirs is not a school with many problems—unlike those with federal funding and a great deal of testing where, she suggests, the need for more constant contact with administration might make sharing more difficult.

They divide time equally during the week, one usually covering staff meetings for both, though Evelyn notes, "I often come in extra because it's part of my feeling of responsibility." Division by areas of personal strength has become natural over the years.

Described by her partner as more "innovative," Laura enjoys talking with the school board and relating to the community. "I'm more creative and spontaneous," she comments. "Evelyn is more organized and doesn't mind tasks that I think tedious, like book ordering and record keeping." Evelyn herself adds, "Paper work and routine jobs are kind of fun."

In the beginning year or so, they tended to overlap at least one day, but gradually turned to notes and frequent phone calls to maintain communication. Both feel strongly about the difference between part time work and sharing, even though (unlike classroom teachers) they don't need to cover for each other for sick leave days. They have, however, become accustomed to a sense of mutual support.

"We have a lot of decisions," Laura explains, "about handling our budget, for example, and I know that non-sharing reading teachers are jealous because we can discuss problems and bounce ideas. We've learned a lot from each other with our different professional backgrounds and family responsibilities . . . I'm kind of emotional and worried about the teachers and Evelyn has a much more mature perspective."

Evelyn describes their sharing as a "tremendous opportunity to learn from each other. It's hard to get feedback from teachers when you're alone. They're inclined to tell at least one of us and we can evaluate programs better together. It gives you more confidence when you can collaborate."

Each feels that their combination makes them more effective employees. "I figure we work 120 percent," says Laura, "not only 'cause I'm manic when I'm there because I think I'm not going to be back tomorrow. I don't sit and chat after school and rarely have lunch. It's not just that we work well together, but that we have to be more efficient when we're there and have more energy. We've introduced programs that other reading teachers haven't been able to."

They've also collaborated on a book, a combination of their programs and materials, originating, says Evelyn, "from Laura's enthusiasm and ambition." They are proud that the text on teaching of reading was well reviewed and that its sales are increasing.

After four years of working together, each is aware of different stresses, more with the scope of their work than with the partnership. Evelyn now feels a desire for full time work, wanting greater challenge and needing more income.

Laura admits to the frustration of always wanting to accomplish more. She comments, however, that "working part time isn't just leisure, but time off in other career directions that I wouldn't have time or energy for otherwise." One of these is teaching extension courses for reading teachers at nearby community colleges. "The day I do those is the day I'm home and preparing. By 6:30 I've been home all day and I'm ready to talk to a group of teachers. Once you're locked into a full time job and getting up every morning and being somewhere 8-4, your brain doesn't have the chance to be thinking of anything else. This is a balanced life."

## ADJUSTMENTS: PARTNERS AND JOB CHANGES

*Elementary school teachers probably form the single largest category of job sharers. Many consider the sharing as important as the teaching—the relationship with another trusted adult who could carry a classroom on his or her own. As one explains, "If two people who respect one another's teaching and philosophy can form a partnership of open communication, they're giving their students the best of themselves." Others claim that only the desire to work part time creates shared contracts; this view is explained by a teacher who says, "The choice of a compatible partner is second. If you find such, there are no problems; if you don't, the job may be somewhat abrasive, but in most cases workable."*

*Teachers: Accommodating to Different Styles*

*Ralph and Lucille teach a combined 3rd-4th grade in a district which has recently encouraged more shared teaching. Their school, which receives federal funding for special programs, has a comfortable, informal atmosphere. The principal and staff take advantage of the diversity of staff and student body. Relaxed and enthusiastic about his personnel and program, the principal praises the teaching of this partnership. "As long as you're not uptight about things, they work out," he comments.*

Ralph, in his late fifties, had served as a principal elsewhere for some 20 years but wanted to devote time to family and to new outside interests. "I used to feel that education was the answer to the world's problems," he explains. "I practically lived in my office . . . . I'd be there all day Saturday, most of Sunday, and neglected my family in the process." But, by the time he decided to return to teaching, the situation had changed and even substitute teaching was hard to come by.

"Coming back in the shared position, I've been very fortunate," Ralph says, "first, with a beginning teacher who brought this fresh breeze of new ideas and helped me catch up on new curricular development. And I felt I shared with her some of the things I picked up over the years, like organization structure and behavior modification, which is a nice euphemism for discipline." He and Lucille met just a week before the beginning of school.

"It's interesting," he explains, "how people, whenever they're given an opportunity to respond, will do so willingly. Negative things can be ironed out—unlike a situation that's imposed.'' Before they agreed on the partnership, Ralph remembers the principal saying, ''Lucille and Ralph, here is what we have. Would you like to go into another room and have some coffee?''

''It was just the thing,'' Ralph says. ''We spent an hour talking—felt we could work together, not just for ourselves but for the children. I think she indicated that she'd like mornings and I had no objection. It just came about—a joint decision. Lucille teaches language arts, reading, and spelling in the morning and then I handle math, physical education, science, and history in the afternoon.''

The flexibility is important. ''Lucille is pregnant, you know, and I can cover for her doctor vists, and times when I've had to get away early, no problem,'' Ralph comments. ''I let her know early enough, ask if it would be convenient. No problem. It really puts that little oil into the machinery.

''As I told Lucille, shared teaching is the next most intimate relationship to marriage, and you really get to know each other during the year. The whole thing rests on the compatibility of the two partners, on their communication and flexibility. We both, I think, had to give and take a little, our personalities, our ages . . . the adjustment that I had to make because, let's face it, a person who's 25 or 30 just sees things differently from one who's 55. I tend to be pretty structured. Lucille is a fine disciplinarian. Many young teachers today have a different approach, more of a counseling approach, indirect and so forth, and it works with many children. So we kind of worked out a common ground on discipline and were pleased to find that even though our ages are different, we agree on common academic and conduct standards.

''Usually the first year that a teacher shares, regardless of age or background, there's a time period of shifting from 'I' to 'us' and 'my' to 'our.' This is something that basically has to be overcome,'' Ralph continues. ''When you're teaching a class all by yourself, there's no need to ask yourself, what am I doing to pass on by way of communication about a child's behavior? It takes a conscious effort to remember to communicate. I wouldn't want to say that everything is peaches and cream because we have different orientations, but there's nothing that we haven't been able to sit down and talk about.

"I think one of the mistakes I made at the beginning was in reflecting my administrative background and my age. It's very easy for us old timers to say, 'now, young lady, let me tell you what we should do,' and I caught myself slipping that way, but Lucille was very gracious and instead of saying, 'we're partners,' she listened. Then I'd think about it later, 'now, really, that wasn't the way to discuss it. If we're partners, I should let her have a chance to voice her thoughts more.' So I've been working on that point, to be sure that I don't dominate; or, you might say, hog the show. So, it's been a learning experience for me in respecting someone else's professional judgment."

Lucille, who had been teaching only a few years, was anxious to become part time. She was expecting her first baby and explains that, "last year wasn't the easiest. I was tired and becoming a little disillusioned . . . we had a few discipline problems. The district knew we each wanted part time. The pressure was there . . . but we did click more or less. He was congenial and easy to talk to. They really should give you more time to get acquainted, though.

"For us, it was relatively easy to organize responsibility. He teaches his subjects. I call them his and mine . . . our two areas of curriculum don't overlap. We really don't plan lessons together. Math is just completely separated from reading and language arts, although history could be in with language arts, which might even be a good idea. But we really haven't sat down *per se* to try. It wouldn't be difficult. You know, I had certain things in mind that I want to try and get across.

"I'm super excited about sharing; I've really enjoyed the experience. I really enjoy just teaching half of the curriculum and not being responsible for the whole gamut of subject matter. It's not really part time, more two-thirds. I think teaching a full day is like working time-and-a-half. Sharing is less work because you are sharing common problems and someone else is working on it, whether it's calling a parent or anything else. I've told other teachers, when they see me leaving at 12:30 and they look at me with envy, that the few hours free are worth half a pay check. Those two and a half hours when I'm not working are really like five hours because teaching can really be very tiring physically and mentally . . . being in a classroom an extra two and half hours takes its toll. Plus, during that time, even if I go right home after lunch and begin working at home, it's not the same thing as teaching in the classroom. And coming home at four o'clock after teaching all day, the last thing I really want to do is prepare for the next day, correct papers for the day ahead. Yet, it has to get done if you don't want to really get behind, and I'm very conscientious about getting the work done.

"We don't plan lessons together. We do talk a lot about behavior problems or learning problems. We do discuss how that child is functioning—whether we're seeing similar patterns and how we can help. We've really had to get together on discipline to make sure that our methods are consistent, so that if the children have one set of rules in the morning, they don't have a completely different set of rules in the afternoon. Although, I'm sure the morning are a bit more lax. Ralph is more of a disciplinarian than I am by nature, by personality. I've come to appreciate his way of handling situations. He's really well organized and he's able to perceive a problem before it actually happens. So, I appreciate all this. It makes my job easier.

"I believe the children do benefit 100 percent. They have two fresh people every day. I come in in the morning and I'm feeling good and I'm ready to start the day off. By 12:00, especially in my condition now, I've had it. And Ralph comes in and he's ready to go and has not had to handle any problems or know of any problems in the morning and he's ready to take them on and do his best."

*School Librarians: Same Partners, Second Job*

*"They knew several things that people usually don't know until that first year," explains a high school principal who hired two women with job sharing experience for a librarian position. "They*

*knew they could stand each other and that neither would take advantage.* "

Connie and Janet had held a similar job in a nearby school district and had been rehired for the following year. The first experience had been challenging; the school had been without a librarian for some time and they successfully wrote budget proposals and worked on centralizing materials. But regulations in the first district stipulated that, to advance on the pay scale, both partners must be present daily. The commuting they found was time consuming. When an opening came up in their local area, Janet, who had been employed previously in this district, did the initial interviewing for the second position. Because neither partner wanted to change to full time, Janet recalls, "we sort of pledged to share the next job."

Both are in their thirties and hold master's degrees in library science. As mothers with six children between them, they had wanted to continue in their professions, but not as temporary hires or as substitutes, the only opportunities available to them prior to their sharing.

"I wanted to be a librarian," says Connie, "and a part time librarian isn't doing much of a job. That's a librarian that isn't going to be working much longer as far as I can see. I wanted a good library and a good job and it seemed ideal to share."

"I wanted to work in my profession," Janet repeats, "and I needed the flexibility of free time and more than just a part time job."

This vacant position at the high school, explained the principal, had been a difficult spot historically. "I knew I had a problem; we needed more supervision in what had become a pressured atmosphere with 1,500 kids using the library daily." He was intrigued and impressed by the pair when they met together. "This job," he adds, "is one in which a person needs to have time to back away for a day. Unlike a research atmosphere, this is energy consuming because librarians tend to see themselves as disciplinarians, even though they'd prefer to be otherwise."

The fact that they were willing to spend time during the summer to get ready proved a bonus. In addition, the district is one which has been encouraging teachers for some years to share, recognizing special individual needs and anxious to have new hiring wherever possible while facing declining enrollment. Since its initial acceptance of shared jobs, the administration has insisted on the support of immediate supervisors of each particular team as a pre-condition.

"They told us to do the job," said Janet, "and we decided how to cover it." Both feel equally responsible for the total job: operation of the library and study hall, supervising two aides, purchasing materials, and special instructions for incoming students. Alternating two and three days weekly, they divide many tasks, having learned after their initial sharing experience that there was no need to check each other continually.

"We make a stronger librarian together," Janet comments. They came to realize that many decisions could be deferred for later collaboration. "It's often better that way," Janet notes. "If I were working alone I'd feel compelled to rush a decision and that's not necessarily the best way."

Connie acknowledges that she tends to be more hurried and has become much better at working "than if I'd been working on my own because I have her praise, criticism, and suggestions in everything I do. And I do trust her. You really do grow and learn to cooperate."

Careful organization and communication mark their style. "It forces us to be more efficient," says Connie. They use a daily log, notebooks and even "policy cards and procedures," which they felt were necessary because of supervising other aides. "We feel responsible to make it easier for them," explains Connie. Both partners are conscious of the need to inform not only each other but the rest of the staff and to attend most meetings. "They've attempted," notes the principal, "in fact, have leaned over, to be part of the full time program."

"I think we're here (together) more than any one teacher, but we don't feel we have to be," Connie says. Sensitive to possible resentment of their flexibility, Janet comments that, "because you're working half time and you feel you can give more, it may make others feel as though they're not doing as good a job because they're one person—that's not true and that's not right. We think we need to do a lot of public relations with the faculty and the rest of the administration. Some are delighted and others worry about why one isn't on at a particular time."

While the principal acknowledges minor difficulties such as keeping both aware of occasional sensitive areas, he credits the pair with assuming responsibility for informing each other. They themselves have agreed not to take their own problems to him, though each comments differently on whether their performance is judged individually.

"We can remove our own personality," Connie says, "because we're speaking for both of us." Janet elaborates, "We feel that we represent one another, but we also find that students, faculty, parents, and the administration realize that we're two different people and they react differently to each of us. We sometimes feel our different personalities work to our advantage and others will probably find this too in time."

It might surprise the pair that the principal sees the differences in their personalities as part of their strength as a team. He feels that they are an especially good match and attributes the lack of certain supervisory problems to the fact that he was directly involved in their hiring.

"These two have been outstanding," he says, "doing more than any one person could, even if I had the world's greatest. Because they're working as they want, less than full time, and together," he concludes, "they're not watching the clock to the same extent that a full time employee often is. Since they cover for each other rather than call in substitutes, there is a lot of advantage to us; we probably have many fewer days that we pay extra for. Many others, even as pairs, couldn't do as well as these two."

Sharing and Organizational Needs

*Legislative Assistants: Schedule Overlap*

*"We need to open minds to what the employer really needs; in my case, peak coverage during certain hours. Is it necessarily always eight hours daily?" asks a state assemblywoman who hired two women to be her assistants in order to get the best resources for a demanding legislative schedule. She acknowledges that, even as the sponsor of part time employment measures, she was doubtful at first that part time help would suit her own office. Although the two women who applied for the position were willing to work full time, they preferred more flexibility and she decided to hire both to work together.*

*In the years since the job was first shared, there have been many partners. After one member of the original pair left, the other, who remained to train a new partner, commented: "It's possible to have on-the-job training when you have a job sharing situation." At the time of the interview this partner had just left; her second partner remained with a partner who became the fourth sharer. Despite this turnover, the legislator explains, "I still have two heads, time, and talent. I get a better quality person and one supplements the other."*

Beth, one of the first partners who shared for two years, had formerly been a teacher. She had retired from teaching to "do 10 years as mom" to three children. Active in local politics, she had come to know the community well and had gained experience with budgeting matters. Lois, who is younger, married but childless, was more experienced in state and federal government. She had worked for several years as a claim representative in the Social Security Administration. Feeling both she and her husband were working too much, she was glad to work part time.

The partnership has a specially tailored time arrangement to meet the needs of legislative sessions. Both partners work three-fourths time when the legislature is in session and half time or less the rest of the year. "When I'm really busy," the assemblywoman explains, "in a sense, I have two full time people; when I'm not, they aren't here with nothing to do." For a time each had one day off, worked six to eight hours on other days, and divided night meetings. They developed a carefully logged chart to bank time, showing hours worked each week, units accumulated, and minimum units required for half time totals.

Tasks are less well delineated. "It's difficult to describe," says Lois, "because in so many ways it's nebulous."

"Primarily," Beth adds, "our job is to be an extension of the legislator, extra ears, bodies. If each of us can get to different meetings, for example, she essentially made it to three meetings."

"There are so many facets to her job," Beth says, "multiple constituencies among institutions—city, university, school districts, county—all in this district and one institution bumping another."

They also follow her varied committee assignments, one more involved with budget and special committees than the other. They both can fill in, not necessarily on technical expertise, but, says Lois, "we try to know each other's areas. We collaborate and check, and the assemblywoman tends to look to one or the other of us for different types of information."

There's no question that each feels responsible for more than half the job. "If sharing means a person with separate responsibilities," Lois explains, "or half a full time job, and if pairing means responsibility for 100 percent and working it out together, I guess I'd say it's more pairing. We work separately but still collaborate. I need to handle other areas when Beth is away, and be knowledgeable."

They learned to be careful not to duplicate, but with sufficient overlap time, feel no need for formal communication logs.

"One of the chief satisfactions," says Beth, "comes from being able to pick out areas in which one can do best or will develop expertise." Lois adds, "We can relieve each other. It's nice to know that you can rely on someone else when your energies run out . . . their expertise. I think that exists in full time too, but here it's built into the job."

Both speak of mutual support. "I can think of being uncertain in my own response to a given problem," Beth comments, "and being able to turn to Lois and, if she questions it, then I can set off in a different way, or if she supports it, I'm doubly sure I'm right."

Trusting one another to be responsible comes with experience working together over a period of time. In a job with as many changes in partners as this, the incumbent can be keenly aware of comparisons. "You do need the feeling that the other is responsible so that your day off is really off," says Lois.

They find adjustments to be relatively minor. Lois points out, "As long as we can work together and get things done, I don't feel offended by a partner doing things better than I. If we have two people who click and work well together, it doesn't become more than full time which it would be otherwise."

Whatever stresses there are result more from the particular job than from sharing. "If I had kids I would be more torn by irregular hours," Lois feels. "I think I'd want fewer ifs in my life." Beth, who had not worked full time for many years, finds it difficult to make comparisons.

"What made this work so well for us," Lois says, "was the commitment of both of us to the job, which is basically a commitment to our employer. We are treated as adults in the employment relationship and there's no question of our sense of responsibility." Both feel that staff support has contributed to their own sense of satisfaction and effectiveness. They are conscious of being models or, as Beth explains: "This is like the synthesis of part time, because here's a legislator who's trying to promote the concept and who's also doing it as an employer . . . so everybody's looking."

## Health Educators: Contrasting Expectations

*Two young women were hired to create a new position within a small cooperative organization and resigned in frustration after a few months. Their experience exemplifies the difficulties which arise when expectations of the team differ markedly from those of the organization. In this case, both partners had chosen the shared job in the hope that it would prove less demanding than the full time positions which they had held previously. In contrast, the staff of the organization were accustomed to voluntary (non-paid) overtime in jobs which apparently fulfilled a sense of dedication.*

"One of their problems," explained Donna, their supervisor, "was having to function in an unclear setting. And that was a major problem because the organization was just getting itself together. It would be good for job sharing to have the job fairly specifically defined, which this one wasn't. I know it wasn't easy for them. And I can relate to that personally. It's not easy here.

"We really hired them to create the job, so nobody else really knew what to expect. It might have been a mistake to hire someone who had never filled the role before. We thought of that as a strength because they both had specific skills that we were looking for. We didn't want a traditional blinders-on-the-eyes type educator but what they had to do was go back and learn what an educator does in order to go through it. We thought both of their experiences made it a very unique combination. So, it's not job sharing so much as it's a lesson to be learned."

Almost from the time they started the job, Marie and Helen found it easier to organize responsibilities between themselves than to deal with the rest of the organization, including their supervisor.

"She was pretty good about reinforcing what we had decided," Marie said. "I think what we experienced was that it's been hard for her to let go of the bases she covered before we came. There was no clear direction or a sense of trust. It was hard to find where we really belonged. We would go around with our job descriptions trying to educate people about who we were and what we were there to do."

"I don't think I had the expectation," her partner explained, "that I would come into a ready made team, because I've never had that experience. But I had the expectation that the energy would be there to create that. One of the things we were told in our job interviews was that one of the reasons we were hired was because we had experience in bringing teams about. It felt like the very thing we were hired for was the very thing they resisted most strongly." Many co-workers felt committed to doing their own job, rather than working together as the partners had assumed.

Both Marie and Helen felt they lacked the authority to develop programs. "Authority should be commensurate with responsibility; it's not here in this organization," says Marie. "It's all mucked up by 'this is a cooperative—everybody's equal.' " Instead of developing programs, they found it necessary to concentrate on building support within the organization.

"We weren't doing the job we were hired to do," said Helen. "What we were doing was putting a lot of energy into organizational development and into creating the base to do the job. What we started to do (after three months) was to relate our experience around different points in the job description and point out why it didn't work out. That raised the broader issues in the organization that got focused on us because we were the ones that raised the issues."

A part of their problem appears to have been the number of people on the staff, many of whom were working part time too.

"It took twice as long to get to know everyone," their supervisor explained. "I guess I feel that coordinating required that they each know all the people . . . . It isn't like you're going to do this part and I'm going to do that part. They each have to know the total job in a way that they had to know these people."

The partners sensed inconsistencies between principles and practice.

"I think the longer we were involved," Marie said, "the more we experienced these inconsistencies and what effect they had on working with other people in the organization on that cooperative level. As a coordinator, it's assumed that you're going to be doing things with other people. It's not a one-to-one kind of thing. It's pretty hard to provide programs if only one person shows up. It's a doomed role to do your own thing because your own thing required coordination and cooperation. We attempted to do some things without much support and what happened was nobody showed up. A lot of people had a long history in the organization, and ours was very short. We were bucking history as well as the present situation.''

They and the supervisor soon realized the need for more structure, for clear identification of problems and for account-ability.

"I think more of it was that they weren't honest with themselves or with us about the kind of job they really wanted,'' the supervisor says. "I think they wanted a nine-to-five job that was really structured. They were turned on by what we were doing, but that's not the work environment that they wanted—where things were uncertain. I think they would do very, very well at IBM or a very structured setting where the job was well defined. What I got from both of them is that they really wanted to limit their energy, wanted to limit their input. And that was not possible. I feel that was not realistic on their part. They bought our ideals and stuff.''

She credits both with communicating well with each other and the organization. That there were two individuals meant more need for continuity and flexibility—especially for extra meetings.

"They did put in a lot of extra time on their own.'' As their official supervisor, she felt that there were communication problems which were more related to the organization setting than to the two sharers *per se*.

"I really have to say,'' she remembers, "that so much of it is our state of development. We're operating very much on what we'd call 'crisis management.' I think the bigger problem was all the part time staff and not really having them prepared for that.''

Both Marie and Helen then took additional part time jobs, one as a waitress and the other as a nurse. The supervisor felt this was one reason they showed a "whole lack of energy'' in spite of their initial enthusiasm.

"All of a sudden I saw them working at outside jobs," the supervisor says, "and tired and not having energy and not wanting to come to a nighttime meeting. That kind of thing then was very demoralizing for everybody else. I know they were dealing realistically with funding which might not continue. The money was guaranteed for six months, but when they were hired we certainly told them that the position was important to the organization.

But the partners found their second jobs were more rewarding personally. Other staff in this organization, it seemed to them, had an "incredible investment," were working well beyond regular hours, and expected them to do twice their share as well.

"That's their whole life," said Helen. "That can be a handicap in some ways for job sharing."

As the frustrations at work continued and others seemed not to focus on their problems, the partners tended to fall back more on each other for mutual support.

Helen commented, "Had I been alone I would have been pretty wiped out in terms of what I could do—my own sense of competency. Wondering if I'd get a good recommendation."

Her partner sensed "some resentments about our relationship, and that we stuck together no matter what. We were committed to working it out with each other and that was distressing to people when they were feeling their own chaos and they didn't feel that kind of support for themselves."

The supervisor recognized their need for mutual support but also claimed that it had interferred, to some extent, with their receiving organizational support. "If they hadn't had anyone else to talk to, they would have talked to either the supervisor or a particular staff member. Pretty soon they sat there and they talked to each other about the problems in the job which made it kind of . . . they didn't force the organization to deal with their needs. And what we were hoping was that they would help us focus."

*Assistant Editors: Combining Skills*

*In this example, one partner comments: "With Kathy being a school teacher and my being a librarian, we realized that we'd be better off pooling our complementary skills rather than pairing up with a partner of like background."*

*Kathy and Frances share an entry level assistant editing position in a small publishing company. In their twenties and thirties, both are married and have young children. They met at a Job Sharing Workshop, where they discovered a mutual interest in "part time work with a purpose." They decided to apply together for a full time position in a publishing company. Each wrote a separate résumé and together they composed a joint cover letter. At the time of this interview, the team had been working together for nine months.*

"The first time we applied, we definitely found it was the job sharing that was being interviewed and not us," Kathy remembers. "And it was easy. We had prepared all these answers and no one ever asked us any important questions, like benefits, and how you would do this or that."

"I don't think I would have put the time and effort into putting two part time people together," their supervisor, Brad, says in explaining why he selected them from over 90 applicants. "There were enough full time people who wanted the job. If somebody really wanted the job but only wanted to work part time, I probably would have eliminated him. Maybe we were just willing to try something different. Jobs can be boring. This was an opportunity to do something creative at very little risk. I felt it had potential for maximum gain. My boss may have thought this was a crazy idea, but he tolerates exercising crazy ideas if they make money for him."

"Of the four applicants that I asked back," Brad says, "it came down to the job sharing team or this other individual applicant. There was one criterion that was important—that was that we were going into a project that was going to be high pressured and demanding. I was not sure that the one individual applicant was strong enough to withstand that, or any one applicant. I was concerned not about work load but more psychologically. That was the one most significant determining factor in my choosing the job sharing team.

"We had no problem on mechanics," he points out. "When the bookkeeper called me up and asked me how do we work this, I said, 'Kathy and Frances are like one single applicant. Deduct whatever needs to be deducted and they get two checks. The salary just goes two ways.' As soon as I said we just have one full time applicant, we don't have two part time people, it came very clear to her. It's not that complicated."

The first project was clearly defined.

"When we started to write for the catalogue, that was the first time we had to 'put out,' " Frances says. "A lot of the pressure was from within us to live up to an image that we created for ourselves. It was very easy to divide. Kathy wrote one subject and I wrote the other. We didn't overlap at all there. Even some days when we worked together we didn't communicate. Each of us individually felt so much pressure from the date hanging over our heads that on the days we did work we hardly spoke. We would seldom take any kind of break. She would go get coffee and automatically bring me some back and vice versa. It was like that for about a month . . . we got a lot done."

"That pace was difficult," Kathy comments. "It was good in some ways because it was a very short day. I really feel that you offer more in terms of productivity when you're there for a shorter period of time."

For their supervisor it meant: "There were two of them to commiserate—if nothing else but to share some of the burden. I was much freer about applying pressure if I thought it could be evenly distributed between two people. I felt better about sitting across the desk and putting out a negative message to two of them because I thought the two of them would compare notes and would then say, 'yeah, I think he's right,' or 'no, he's not right—he's chewing us out.' They would bolster each other, as I wanted them to bolster each other, in times of stress."

Kathy and Frances have experimented with different time schedules. They began by working half days, then changed to dividing the week by full days after a few months. "I honestly feel our efficiency has gone down," Frances says, "or our productivity, because we are working full days rather than half days. You get into the same rut nine-to-five employees get into. But when we're there for half days we found that we didn't have one day to ourselves . . . always coming into work and three hours here and three hours there." "So now," Kathy adds, "we've gotten to the point where we work two and a half days a week, with overlap either over the phone or notes. That's not as effective as when we're both in the office at the same time. In fact, we've been discussing how to get back to that. We feel a certain obligation to do well and prove that the job sharing can make it."

After finishing their first publication project, they were not immediately reassigned. This created a sense of frustration because they were uncertain about their responsibilities and position and saw themselves as "floaters."

"You can write articles if you like or you may work with another feature writer," Kathy says, " . . . come up with something you would really like to do. It sounded ideal, but as time has gone on, no matter how we ask or push, no one seems to know what's going on."

"The one thing that I think has been good about our sharing in this kind of frustration," Kathy asserts, "is that we both sense it. I think if I were a single employee in this particular bind, I would hold it in or think, 'Gee, is it me?' Also, we have a little more of a push inside to do something about it. On my own, I might not feel that way. I might just either hang on there for the paycheck and hope or just quit. This way I feel more positive in that maybe we can pull something off that we'll like and they'll like and it will work."

They had learned to rely on each other.

"We also get along very well, which you really have to do," Frances comments. "Friction can arise very quickly. I think we had one really bad day I remember where I got very upset with her about something. That's the only time I really remember it. You're responsible for the other person. She can't do a crummy job because it's my head as well. You have to think about that, too, which tends to make you do better. There's somebody there who is really checking you. Even if it's all subconscious.''

For the supervisor, sharing had meant that ''they could bring out the best in each other.'' He remarks, ''There's a certain amount of pride involved. I think everybody is at one time going to slough off—they think nobody else is going to find out. It's a matter of pride when you're working closely with somebody else. I think you get the best of both people.''

''I think there is a certain competition in that you want to be as productive as the other person,'' Kathy says. ''We're both strivers. We probably have basically the same push. I think there's just a pressure that you want to succeed and there would be that pressure regardless of job sharing. It would be like that in any job. Perhaps there's more security as a job sharer. Your partner is somebody who really cares and not someone who's just listening to you.''

Neither partner wants to change to a full time position.

''The flexibility of time is what matters to me,'' Kathy says. ''I don't like being told I have to leave the house at 8:15 and be home at 5:45. I don't live my other life like that and I don't feel I want to live my work life like that.'' But both acknowledge that they still feel ''part time'' even as job sharers.

''I felt perhaps we wouldn't be in the situation we are in now if it was just one of us,'' Frances remarks. ''I feel as if it will always be a part time job in the sense that I don't think a job sharer can 'get ahead' or get promoted as readily as a full time person who is there all the time.''

Reviewing perceptions of the advantages and disadvantages for the company, their supervisor notes that: ''they have a common ground of experience, but they have different skills and different experiences which means they bring . . . an aggregate of maybe ten years or more of experience. That is just a pool of information to draw upon; it's an excellent source to have.''

But he also admits that communication can be a problem occasionally because of lapses among all three, and also because of excesses. Since all three shared a small office he became annoyed by overhearing conversations when they all worked at the same time.

"This job sharing team worked out very well," he says. "But despite all my good feelings about it, there are some limitations. I think you can only go so far with it. While the two in a team tend to bolster one another, to spur one another to better efforts, there's a high level and a low level. They tend to operate toward the higher level, but I think inherently the job sharing prevents them from soaring above that high level into that superior level. I found myself limiting my interaction with them because I wanted it to be equal interaction with both members of the team. I found that the limitation all the way through this experience has been my desire to keep the communication, the degree of involvement, the degree of enthusiasm, equal with both members of the team.

"I suppose by emphasizing cooperation and emphasizing a productive team," he said, "I tend to dampen those flights of maximum output that any one individual can experience. I could have been very production oriented and looked at them as sources of raw material and thought that the best way to get the most out of these people is to set them against each other. I don't tend to manage that way. Personal relationships are more important to me than the bottom line on a productivity chart."

Since the time of the interview, the team has been promoted to permanent staff status.


STYLES OF COOPERATION: COORDINATORS AND DIRECTORS

*City Organization Development Consultants:*
*Partnership Differences*

*In a city which originated job sharing in 1975, primarily to encourage affirmative action hiring, Pat and Bruce work together as internal organization development consultants. Theirs is one of*

*the unusual higher-salaried jobs, the only really "team" job (of*
*the 7 shared positions in the city) envisaged as such by the*
*personnel department. In filling the new position, the city had*
*sought to combine the expertise of two individuals in order to get*
*the greatest variety of skills to reach out to all city departments.*

"To other city governments," says the personnel director, "job
sharing seems to have some mystique that to me isn't there.
There's a lot of common sense involved, not a magic formula.
You can see the advantages and the disadvantages and I guess
some people think there must be a lot more to it than that. You
know it can be whatever you want it to be. You know you can
analyze the cost of any new position, but what it's going to give
you—that's not so easy to determine."

"I thought it was a little unusual," says Pat, "for the city to
have a full time job but persist in getting two people to share; the
concept of job sharing was something I wasn't familiar with." She
had previously worked only full time and had recently moved to
this city. When the administration arranged to interview
applicants singly and in a variety of pairs, as arranged by the city,
Pat was surprised.

"It really struck me how innovative the city was," she
remembers, "and by the time I got through the interview process,
even though I had wanted a full time job, I wanted to work for this
organization."

Her partner also had been full time before, working in large
private organizations. He was interested in working for a public
agency but, in order to continue his private consulting business,
wanted only a part time commitment.

"One of my requirements," says Bruce, "was that I didn't have
to accept a particular partner. We met again after we were selected
and talked a few hours and I didn't accept the job until then. We
both had concerns about how the sharing would actually work
out, how we could give each other support, etc. One of the minor
adjustments at the beginning was to decide on how to divide the
work. This was a change, because I was used to making decisions
independently. If I didn't want a task before, I gave it to other

people. It wasn't a big issue. While we have different styles, we see the professional world pretty much the same way."

The job lent itself to division of responsibilities for specific city departments and to collaboration in areas involving overall functions.

"We overlap in several ways," Pat explains. "For example, in terms of what the philosophy of the job is going to be. If we are off working in different parts of the organization, we still have to adhere to the same values to have the kind of impact we want. So we have to talk a lot about what is important to do and not to do; what types of things we want to preserve and what we want to change. We have to talk about us taking responsibility in each department—you know, whether you are taking too much responsibility or whether we are being used in other ways. We also overlap in working with the top management team on goals and evaluation of the programs. So both of us should have access to that kind of information."

They recognize a need for mutual support but have different emphases.

"One of the things that is very difficult," says Pat, "is an overload of information. Most of the people who talk to me talk about problems which could be depressing. They tell you things and they want the information to get represented, but discreetly. I bank all this information while I listen to managers' problems and I see myself as an interpreter. Now the problem, being in the middle, is whom do I tell? I have so much information I have a headache. Bruce is the only person in the organization I really feel free to share it with. I think we'd both prefer to overlap more."

Bruce views collaboration as an extra.

"Collaboration isn't necessary, but it enriches," he explains. "Our business, organizational development, is very unique. To a large extent our job is change and there is a lot of resistance. If people feel threatened, they can accuse us of crummy work, so in that sense it is important that we both do well. We're dealing with people's feelings as influenced by objective occurrences within the organization. The more one knows of them, the more one can appreciate their views, but it isn't necessary. We can each do a super job without seeing each other. Pat and I have worked out styles that leave us independent. We can get by for weeks without seeing each other and it doesn't interfere with the quality of the work we do. We have tried, though, to build into our schedules time to get together each week so we can keep each other up to date on what we are doing and review our ideas and plans. We don't always make it every week, but when we do it is very helpful.

"What is essential is what we give to each other as professionals. In a way I am spoiled because I came from a place where I had worked with many professionals with whom I had a lot of contact. I kept updated and touched bases on common stresses. This job is a dramatic change and I miss that professional contact. It helps to have Pat around. There would be no other way to meet the need."

The personnel director sees the partners as having distinct perceptions of their roles in the organization. "It is difficult to avoid comparing them," he says. "One is more of a consultant, which the position lends itself to. Not that one approach is better. If you're not committed you can be suspect; if you're too committed you can get too close and lose perspective."

To a certain degree, Pat and Bruce differ on the importance each attaches to the need for accessibility by the rest of the city staff.

"I have a schedule over here and people will call and find out where I am. I'm pretty accessible," says Pat. "I really feel strongly that people should know where I am because sometimes a manager will call and say, 'I have a woman who's hysterical and I know you're not working today, but she'll be here at 7:00—I don't think I can face her then.' You know, if it's possible, then I go over there at 7:00. It's very hard to say that I'm only going to be here Monday through Wednesday, but I discipline myself as much as possible. One of the things I learned from Bruce is there's a lot of value in keeping yourself removed from the organization.

People tend to get close to me; that's part of me as a person. I have learned to keep a certain kind of distance from everyone in the organization. Bruce doesn't have that problem.

"Another part of the problem," she continues, "is that I have a lot of energy for this job. It could be more than what's necessary, and that makes us more of a contrast. And yet our differences are not that big. I have a lot of respect for his opinion. I did have to learn to collaborate, having consulted on my own in the past, and I learned about my own strengths and weaknesses by collaborating."

Bruce sees the time commitment as more limited. "My real adjustment was to working only half time. It was terrible—I was getting a 20-hour paycheck and working 45 hours a week. I realized that I had fallen into it and I decided to cut back. When we first started, Pat and I decided not to work an absolute work schedule. We decided that it didn't matter; we would do what's comfortable. But I had to control my time. To do so, I decided I wouldn't be caught dead in this place Monday or Tuesday. My clients know that if they want to reach me, they have to schedule the other days. I rarely get calls at home. Once a manager called me on a crisis and I both appreciated and resented it. It's my private time."

Bruce feels he brings more to the job, not only because of his outside consulting, but because he is less involved in the "internal garbage" than full time people are. "If you're going to make it on a part time basis," he explains, "it's probably helpful that you don't need to look to the organization for your social needs, but to the rest of your life—other job, people, and family. If any individual has a history of getting his or her social needs met on the job, then working only half time is not going to be satisfying."

Their supervisor acknowledges some problems of coordination with the partners and of distinct personality differences, but is keenly aware of advantages to the city.

"First," he explains, "it allows two types of professional approaches to the position, gives us the luxury of two strengths and also the luxury of ganging up on certain situations, when both are involved with top management problems. If we had only one, we might have to contract with somebody to come in from outside. They overlap well. Also, it allows them to keep current in their profession, which is an advantage not only to them but to the city because it keeps them sharp in terms of the time we get. Another thing is that Bruce and Pat don't only work 20 hours. It's hard for anyone to discipline themselves to work only 20 hours. Now we don't require or encourage it—their time just fills up. Sharing does cost more, but it's not a significant amount. In essence, we're paying medical premiums twice. Retirement contribution is a function of salary so it is no more. As a public agency, we pay into the public employee retirement system, but not social security.''

Bruce sums up his feelings about job sharing and philosophizes on the criteria for successful extension for others.

''On the question of cost effectiveness of job sharing, I'm here half the time and I, for the most part, am pumped up, turned on, and ready to go on hitting it. In other jobs I have had, 40-hour jobs, I'm either coming up or going down part of the time. I think that any job in any organization can be designed to be shared, but what it means is that people who relate to it have to believe that and buy into it. If an organization anticipates things, it can deal with them. Organizations who say they can't do it are simply saying they have never done it. You have to think about how to do it differently. For a lot of managers it's not worth it to gamble. It only works if the organization is prepared to change the norm of full time where you have to be seen to be working 60 hours a week. It has to be a conscious decision and you have to use a different yardstick for success.''

''This is a better arrangement,'' Pat concludes, ''with two people in it, because one person would have too limited an access to reach people in all departments, and especially because it's a new job. It had to be designed and developed, and people had to be educated to our functions and how to use them. It's better with two because so much is associated with each personality where some people prefer each one. Some would rather deal with a white male than a black female, though ten years from now it might be different. We both have full responsibility for the total job, and this job is easier to share than others even at this level. In this job, it's good because people would be hard put to say what is supposed to come out of it. It is all situational, relative, not measurable, and it is easier and richer because it is split. To me, it narrows down to whether you have hardware or people."

## Program Directors: Success for Whom?

*Grace and Roger shared the leadership of a program for disabled students at a community college. Their example illustrates the difficulties which arise when both partners and the organization are unable to resolve problems of personality differences, expansion of job responsibilities, and ambivalent supervisory support. However, both sharers found the experience valuable. One who eventually assumed full responsibility would not have been likely to achieve this without starting the job with this partner. The other, now employed elsewhere, acknowledges that the shared position provided a transition between being alone at home and his entry into the work world.*

"Initially, job sharing for us was fantastic," Grace remembers. "Our complementary skills and personalities made the position very successful—so successful that it ruined for us the essence of sharing. When the program grew and more staff were added, our different styles of management became a detriment to the organization. When the administration decided that one of us had to be the director, everything that had been shared disintegrated."

Their supervisor explains: "We started to try having two half time people. We ended up having both work more than half time, so in that sense the college benefited from it. It did require double fringe benefits, so it is a more expensive operation. Ultimately, we found it did not work because we could not have dual heads of the program. They weren't checking with one another. They were making decisions in conflict with one another. In a program where you're an information center and are placing people throughout the campus, you really do need some consistency. They're very different people and the job required both of them to be detail persons. The program grew constantly while the pair was working together. A lot of things fell between the cracks. They didn't know what was wrong. They started out liking each other very much and it became less than that. We tried to have them attend staff meetings together—it didn't always work that way. I tried to counsel with them, referee with them.

"They both came to a point where they agreed that one person had to become responsible. I asked them to decide who that should be. Both of them decided that they themselves were the better person. I asked them if they were making me play God and they said, 'yes.'"

The principal advantage of job sharing, in the supervisor's opinion, is that "you're able to use unique contributions of each person, which is almost invariably better than any one person. But, as we at the college get larger it is administratively easier and simpler if we have fewer people—not so many part time people. If a person is full time, he is really committed to his job. It's commitment—it's intangible, but it's there."

Grace, now in her early forties, suffered an accident 20 years ago which had left her a paraplegic. She had attended business school for a year and worked as an executive secretary. After the accident, she said, "I really started rethinking my life and I thought, 'well, I'll never marry and my job will be very important to me,' and I didn't want to sit behind a typewriter all my life, so I made an effort to fund my college education. I went on and got a B.A. and then an M.A. in speech and hearing therapy."

She worked as a therapist for a few years, married and adopted two children, and was "essentially a housewife" for a number of years. After intermittent temporary jobs she worked with a city committee to do a study of architectural barriers of the public buildings.

"It really opened my eyes," she says. "I realized maybe I could do more for the disabled. In the meantime the position here became available—a full time position. When I was on the city committee, Roger was also on the committee and heard about the position opening. He has multiple sclerosis and hadn't been working for a number of years. He wanted the job and I wanted the job and we decided why don't we both apply—neither one of us wanted to work full time.''

About 35 others applied for the job, but only Grace and Roger were unwilling to work full time.

"We were interviewed separately, as individuals, and then we were given the position and it was really fine,'' Grace says. "We each had full time benefits, and it started out beautifully. Our initial job—part of our job—was to increase services for disabled students on campus. The big push has always been to expand the program, so we did a lot of public relations work, going out into the community. There was a lot of publicity—the two of us in wheelchairs and this kind of thing—and we got a lot of coverage from the news media. But the main focus at that time was to organize the program.

"At that point in time, I never thought of myself as a self-assured person. I was half scared about having a job like this and also I thought—'golly, on a college campus with all these intellectuals,' you know. Roger is a public relations kind of guy, so initially it worked out very well because he did all the talking. But I'm better at organization and getting things going in the office and felt comfortable doing that. Quite often we'd go into the community together, and there again he'd do most of the talking or he'd go himself and I'd stay back in the office, and that was kind of a comfortable role. We also co-taught guidance classes, and again he was kind of the leader.

"We tried to alternate days, but both of us were so involved in the job—he would be coming in every day and if I were home a day, he'd call me up and vice versa. At first we were both totally committed to making this program go, and it became very successful. But midway through the year, I started thinking of some of the things he said that I don't really agree with. It was sort of the same role I had all these years, sort of secondary to the male figure. So as time went on, I started being a little more assertive. Things deteriorated a little bit. We continued on through that year and it wasn't all that bad, but I realized that we were becoming competitive with one another.''

The program grew very rapidly during the first year, and that also contributed to the disintegration of the job sharing.

"We added all kinds of new staff," Grace continues, "mostly full time. So, the second year, we both accepted a three-quarter time contract. We started in the fall, and early on there was a breakdown in what was happening. The first days are kind of chaotic anyway, but part of it was because we were sharing a job. He'd come in one day and he'd say, 'do this' to the staff, and I'd come in the next day and say 'do that.' I found it difficult communicating with him. Anyway, this was a poorly organized beginning, and after a month we were still not working together and things just fell apart.''

She now feels that there was too much overlap or duplication of services and that "we did not divide up the time well enough. Maybe that was part of the problem. We didn't go off in different directions. I guess neither one of us wanted to miss out on anything. So we'd go to various meetings together. He would come in on his days off to do that; he was so committed. He'd come in even though he wasn't supposed to be there." It bothered her "because I wanted time for me, for my time in the office. Both of us were fledglings—we hadn't had any past experience in this kind of thing, so we just sort of worked together and duplicated services.''

By the end of the second year, it became apparent that one would have to take charge, and Grace took on the role of director. Roger left soon thereafter.

"I think that's an awkward thing when one partner becomes subordinate after having worked as equals," Grace explains. "If it had been reversed, I'm sure I would have felt just as badly as Roger did.

"He added a great deal, and I have to give him a lot of credit for that. He was very innovative. I'm sure I learned a lot from him, and both of us really got this program going. It might have gone off in a different direction had I gotten the job alone. First of all, I don't think I would have had the nerve to want a full time job. I wouldn't have had the self-confidence to get this program going as well at the time I started working."

Roger's memory of the experience varies only a little. In his late thirties, married to a working wife and the father of three children, he had spent several years at home in a wheelchair. He says, "I tried some freelance work, but I certainly wasn't in the competitive job market." He had been immediately interested when the position opened, but because "I wasn't feeling sufficiently good about myself, nor sufficiently strong enough to take it on single-handedly, I asked Grace if she wanted to share it on a 50-50 basis. I felt that two different people with two different disabilities would be able to relate more to the heterogeneous student body."

At first, he remembers, they worked well together.

"We were 'interchangeable,' " he says. "Of course, it wasn't super planned out, but catch as catch can. We divided on our interests, mine in public relations with community and campus, hers in the details of registration. The counseling was left open for students to decide."

Uncertain as to whether they learned from each other, he said, "She'd been disabled a lot longer than I had and had certain perceptions of things and means of coping. I suppose there was a little learning in that." He feels confident that she learned from his skills, an awareness of press possibilities and public speaking, for example. But he adds, "I can't speak for her."

"The difficulties came when the program exploded—we had been so busy just coping." They also needed more space, facilities, and help. "We were not sufficiently encouraged in our cooperation," Roger said. "We didn't get enough time when it was needed.

"Our relationship," Roger said, "deteriorated into reasonable peaceful existence. You're sharing a job but you're not sharing the same attitudes and you're not sharing the same criteria for a successful performance." He enjoyed working overtime, but felt that it contributed to the uneveness.

"Shared jobs," he feels, "are ideal for a certain segment of the population that really needs them, and that's disabled people— people in reentry roles whose self-esteem or confidence has waned and who really are not ready to go out and compete in the marketplace for a job. It offers them kind of a tentative half step back which may be the first step in a long successful journey into the kind of thing they want to do. They're not in a good place to do it on their own initially."

### Co-Directors: A Philosophy for Practical Growth

*Co-directors of a special university program, Brenda and Ray share responsibility for facilitating collaborative research between the university and the local community. They work with 85 community groups who request assistance, with 300 students and an equal number of faculty members in order to organize some 100 projects yearly. Their job involves continuous coordination— from the initiation of requests and assistance during process, to final completion for students' academic credit.*

*Hired by a policy board of students and faculty, the partners are technically employees of the university. During the last three years, they have developed various styles of working together in order to adjust to an expanding program and to maintain their personal needs for free time and for their commitment to collaborative work.*

Brenda, who has a master's degree in education, found that her original career plan had become obsolete and became active in community volunteer work. As the mother of young children, she had sought part time positions which were all at the assistant level.

"I was usually going to be overqualified," she comments, "and also I had the interest and motivation to try and run something. There weren't any 'running' jobs that were part time."

Ray, her partner, who had received a master's degree in counseling, had at one time worked for the university, but he realized he didn't want to work a 40-hour week. "I wasn't necessarily pursuing a shared position," he explained. The divorced father of two young sons, he had wanted to reduce his financial needs and become involved in developing small scale self-sufficient communities and in neighborhood and community organizations.

At the beginning, both partners made no attempt to divide the tasks of the job in any particular way in terms of time.

"We were particularly sensitive to not work more than the specified amount of time," Ray explains, "because we felt it important that we both be identified as directors of the program. Since we were in contact with different people, it would be very easy for one person to take an apparently predominant role and we thought that could only be divisive."

"When you're just getting started," Brenda comments, "when you're working out who is going to do what and how to resolve the differences of opinion and conflicts that will inevitably arise, if one person is there more of the time, even it it's only a few hours, the psychological difference can be very great. It's important also that you don't fall into the trap, particularly in a job like this where you could always stay extra hours, not to fall into working over your agreed upon time limit. What can easily happen is that one person keeps working just a little bit more and the other feels he has to keep equal and not feel he's shirking, and you can escalate into defeating the whole point of job sharing—which is to protect a certain period of time so you can do something else."

In succeeding years, Ray and Brenda kept their hours equal. They began to divide topic areas and to expand their working hours from half time to larger increments but still less than full time. As the program expanded, remaining interchangeable proved impossible. Recently they decided to work slightly different amounts of time, feeling, as Brenda says, that they had "already developed procedures and patterns that were based on total equality." One reason was so that Ray could qualify for extended fringe benefits.[2] But their general time arrangement remains that Brenda works daily for fewer hours and Ray has one special day away from the office.

"My hours were tied into paid and unpaid child care," Brenda explains, "and I don't have any other choice, but Ray is also protective of his free time." The basic requirements are to see that the office is covered, that partners have sufficient overlap, and that Brenda's family schedule stays flexible.

They are less concerned now than earlier with projecting a team image, but still feel a strong sense of identification with one another. "I think we've both been pleased with the program," Ray says. "We've been comfortable with each other's performance, but there's no question that both of our functioning is critical. If one of us fell down, the whole program would fall down."

Brenda explains the rewards of sharing responsibility as something that "may not happen in the first month, but if you share a job over a period of years, it's kind of like a partnership, where you have someone you can exchange ideas with. As a result you are constantly getting feedback on your good ideas, your bad ideas, your ridiculous ideas. There's someone to challenge you—there's someone for you to challenge. So the vitality within a job is ever so much greater than when you're in it all by yourself, and the likelihood of new ideas and new approaches seems to me to be increased. One of the effects of a shared job is to reduce the feeling of being threatened. You're willing to try the idea of something that's risky, and you know it's risky, but having talked it over and explored every angle, you can mutually decide this is the right thing to do. And one is often willing then to dare a lot more and reach a lot more. If it doesn't work, it doesn't work, but you have arrived at the decision in a collaborative process and somehow that seems a much stronger incentive for me to be an effective leader than when I'm all alone and I have my doubts and there isn't anyone to turn to. Then I tend to have to play that restraining role."

---

2. Benefits are prorated, except that full medical coverage begins with a 30-hour week.

"What has happened," Ray explains, "is that we have had to confer with one another and see that we are doing things that are harmonious and compatible with each other. In a few situations, it has been a bit cumbersome, but we don't just go charging off into the blue without checking with the other. On the other hand—and this was particularly true in the beginning, but even so now—it's a relatively high stress job, and there we have been able to be supportive of each other. In the first year, maybe first year and a half, there were times when things were hard and we could have gotten on each other's cases, but we were really able to stop and reflect and see what the situation was and give each other support while all this was happening."

Competition is less a problem than an incentive for this team which is based on the pooling rather than the matching of skills.

"It isn't something that you solve right at the beginning," Brenda explains. "A little bit of it, actually, I think is quite healthy. Because if you're kind of in a slump, and you're grousing along and then you see someone else is all enthusiastic, or something really goes well and Ray tells me about it, and I feel just a little shot of adrenalin. 'Well, you know, I can do that, too!' In limited doses, it sort of spurs you on to try a little harder. Even though you may be trying a different thing, still you want to be as enthusiastic as the other person. It may help that, to some extent, we have different interests and different skills, and that may also relate to the fact that one's a man and one's a woman. We do find the same kinds of things funny, and that helps a lot. But I think it is important that we are both interested in and good at different things. Perhaps if our interests overlapped more, or if our lifestyles were closer, maybe we would be more competitive—that's possible. I feel Ray brought to the job quite a sophisticated set of skills and knowledge about human interaction. More so than I did. I hadn't studied psychology as much as he had, and I think that I've learned an awful lot from him in terms of communication and conflict resolution."

Both partners agree that open discussion of differences is most important. "We don't take our differences to the board," Brenda says. "It's helped keep us functioning in a healthy and positive way. But I think we're both aware that we do have great differences. We do not see eye to eye on many things and it takes hard and conscious and conscientious work to keep the area of overlap alive and real and meaningful. When we've had real differences, we have put aside everything else and really worked, I mean really worked hard, to explore all the reasons for the differences. Sometimes it's taken us days, and sometimes we'll set aside time outside of work."

Diversifying responsibility, they were conscious of the need to keep each other informed. Use of a daily log helped. But even when both worked only half time, they were careful to overlap at least an hour daily. When work time for each expanded, overlap time did as well. They have also set up a computer based information system.

"I guess that sounds a little bit funny," Ray said, "because it sounds a little distant, communicating through a computer, but I guess what's important is that there be some accessible information on projects for the person who's less familiar with that project—as well as for the overall program. The computer would not be justified just on the basis of our communication."

Ray and Brenda recognize the need to schedule for extra meeting time to avoid the separation resulting from larger physical space and added staff members. They also feel, as Brenda explains, that when two people who are not particularly similar work together over a long period of time, "it's very natural that one becomes good at x and one at y, and that the x and y become further apart."

Their collaborative style carries over to other staff in their office and to the policy board with whom the directors maintain frequent contact.

"I think," says Brenda, "we consciously or unconsciously work to create an atmosphere in which everyone who works here owns the program. Sometimes, when there are differences of opinion, particularly between the two of us, there's a natural feeling that the students who work with us would align themselves with one or another. But what becomes critical then is that the two people who are jointly responsible work it out and that you not get 'allies' on your side.''

Ray reflects that when they hired the first additional staff member, there were lengthy discussions on the need for hierarchy and structure.

"I think, in retrospect, we probably could have made the distinctions clearer than they are, but it's worked quite well.''

Both partners attend meetings, although they questioned whether it is the best use of their time. "It's very important,'' Ray concludes, "that the board see us both as equals and as a unit. The fact that we're two people, if anything, requires less time because we get some support and advice from each other that we don't need from them.''

PARTNERS AT HOME AND AT WORK

*Faculty Couples: A Composite Profile*

The following examples are among the most unusual of all job sharing experiences. Married couples represent only a small proportion of job sharers and, in spite of the perceived advantages to individuals and institutions, they will probably remain few in number. But theirs are also among the most intriguing experiences. In a broad sense, they illustrate the modern version of historical family work sharing—the Mom and Pop business, the family farm, the domestic work units of other generations. They also indicate the complexity of realizing the desire to reestablish the connection between family and work which largely disappeared as paid employment moved from closeknit domestic arrangements to the large, complicated organizational setting.

Job sharing, as experienced by these couples, focuses on the very specific problems posed when both a husband and wife, trained in the same subject area and aimed at the same level in higher education, are unable to find places together in institutions which are both professional and family social settings. Universities and colleges are often relatively self contained units, sometimes isolated geographically as well; one spouse, usually but not always the wife, is likely to be frustrated by the lack of opportunities to utilize professional training. The following is a composite profile of 13 job sharing couples. It sets forth some of the general issues which will be exemplified more specifically in the concluding two individual partnership profiles. Of all job sharers, these married couples must resolve special problems: in obtaining positions, in maintaining separate identities within the position and institution, and in sharing a more complex work-life relationship.

Why do they want to share jobs? Tom, who teaches at a California college with his wife, explains: "When we last went on the job market we did not want to make a major move to a place where both of us did not have a position in the community. There were several ways of solving that problem and job sharing turned out to be the easiest. In other words, we did not begin with a strong commitment to job sharing."

For many couples, sharing came about after one (usually the husband) had already been teaching at the institution. In some of the more recent examples, the woman was appointed first and the husband followed on a separate contract.

A political scientist who shared an appointment with her husband at a midwestern college comments: "We had young children and the job market is limited. Also Frank wanted to reduce his teaching responsibilities so he could write. He had been employed then for three years. I had served as his leave replacement one year . . . we asked for the [shared] appointment the next."

Joan and Larry were jointly appointed as faculty and house residents in an eastern college. They very specifically wanted a shared job and wanted to work together.

"Our skills are similar but complementary," Joan says. "And because work is so integral to our own life, we didn't want to be in separate worlds, but wanted to combine teaching with residential work life.''

Most couples sought less than full time positions in order to have time for research, the sharing of family life, child care, and domestic chores; they turned to sharing as a means of achieving balance without sacrificing their commitment to teaching. Convincing administrators that such arrangements would work, however, is another matter. Although anti-nepotism rules no longer exist officially, the practice of hiring couples in the same institution even for two full time positions still meets with opposition. One difficulty, commom to all job sharers, is the employer's doubt that two individuals can share responsibility and authority. In addition to the commonly perceived organizational complications, there is concern about a married couple's ability to function as independent but cooperative professionals. Furthermore, the usual skepticism about the value of part time work is even more strongly articulated in the academic profession than elsewhere.

"It is clear that it helps considerably to start with an administration that is genuinely interested," explains Tom. "From our own experience . . . if an administration is not interested, it is hard to convince them to see that most problems can be solved."

A major problem, according to a president of an eastern university, is the fear that "the couple will split for some reason, creating an awkward situation for the college, or that one will not perform as expected, thereby forcing consideration of whether or not the entire relationship has to be terminated, thus sacrificing one performer along with one non-performer."

Institutions have dealt with this in a variety of ways. In those few colleges which already have legislated regulations for permanent part time, with prorated benefits and separate tenure track, job sharing becomes more easily arranged. Each individual is treated on his/her merits.

In brief, institutions have developed various types of contracts: separate, linking, or joint; and temporary or more regularized.

Colleges have been concerned about tenure, voting rights, sabbaticals, even the sharing of office space. Couples are worried about the amount of time required to fulfill "half time" arrangements. They have devised various types of schedules: some on alternating semesters, some teaching joint courses, some dividing teaching but collaborating on research. Administrative duties, such as committees and student advising, have been performed separately or together.

Many administrators have found their initial fears to be unfounded. "From the college's point of view," one president says, "we probably enjoy the equivalent of more than one full time person's effort, because each of the part time participants gets drawn in and gives more time and effort than the job definition demands. A second, perhaps more important, advantage is the satisfaction that comes to the participants who can share their lives so fully. A third . . . is in the alternative role and models thus available to students and other faculty."

The dean of another eastern college admits that it does "take a special pair of people and kind of department to do it. We think it is particularly important that we seize ways to adjust to both professional and family needs, as a women's college." Above all, she points out, there must be equal professional competence; in this instance, "they both could be full time if they wanted it."

Couples themselves have real concern over the problem of working more than half time, concern about finances, the future—issues common to all sharers. But these are compounded for some couples by an underlying apprehension that the administration and other faculty may not recognize them as separate entities. One professor fears trading on their "uniqueness . . . as that sharing couple;" another worries about what might happen if he were to look for a full time job on his own once again. Many couples, not sharing but teaching in the same university, fear that they are already jeopardizing professional recognition and therefore advancement.

Only a few couples speak of competition as a potential problem between married partners. More, however, stress the need for time away from the community. They are concerned about the job becoming the center of their life together. "Personally, I find it very hard to make either generalizations or prescriptions," says a job sharing assistant professor. "We had been married nine years when we began to share a job and I do not think this has affected our marriage in any fundamental ways—but I can easily imagine opposite situations. These days I find it impossible to make convincing statements which will cover the strengths and weaknesses of marriages I know or could foresee."

"The touchstone for success," says one wife, "is being aware of our own boundaries, both as individuals and as a pair."

*Business Managers: A New Life Style?*

*Mary and Gordon, a married couple in their thirties, began sharing the position of business manager at a small college recently. The appointment meant a deliberate change in their style of living, Gordon leaving a job in business at twice their combined present salary and his wife working for pay for the first time in years.*

*"Gordon's expertise was impressive," says the president, who was intrigued by job sharing, "and Mary had certain qualities that we needed just as desperately." The school was interested in an affirmative action candidate. "In a student body such as ours," the president noted, "where there has been an awful lot of consciousness raising on the part of women, it's unspeakably fortuitous that we got, for this very difficult job, a woman who is attractive and who can, in a certain sense, be a role model for students."*

"My life was just all out of kilter," Gordon says, "working hard and doing the business trip and not a whole lot else. Mary was getting fed up with my being gone a lot, traveling, being gone emotionally. After moving here, we have done a lot of experimenting in our lives and our relationship that have sort of opened up our awareness for a lot of concerns. And from my standpoint, that was the beginning of realizing that it was important to me to have a relationship with my kids. They were strangers."

Mary wasn't sure she wanted to work at all, but as long as her husband wanted to make the change, she was pleased at the chance to earn a salary of her own.

The couple decided to split the salary to suit their requirements, taxes, and other needs; and benefits they found easily divisible. The time division is such that Gordon works three days and Mary two. He handles the accounting, finances, and budgeting, and she the housing and dining hall operations, each directing separate staff.

"It is stereotyped," explains Gordon, "but it also happens that our particular background was that."

"Some of the things that Mary is doing," the president comments, "Gordon didn't want to do and would, therefore, have not done well if we had had him full time."

Both have the same title. "Gordon's job is very set," Mary says. "Actually, he does the traditional controller things and I'm doing a lot of the extra things that have just been let go before." Her husband notes, however, that she is slowly becoming familiar with his areas of responsibility. "She's sort of learning, sitting in on committees; I'm doing more of the talking." In part, this came about, Mary explains, because she'd begun to feel that she was dealing only with people responsible to her, he with people "above him."

Some of the staff are waiting to see how the arrangement works out and worry about who will be ultimately responsible when it really comes to a "crunch." "A husband and wife team in a small group might cover up for each other," commented one. "You know, you get paranoid over this; I don't think they will ever get that way, but one thinks about it."

The president, however, is pleased with the arrangement. He speaks of freshness and vitality, and feels that the couple keeps each other informed so that each is answerable pretty much for the other.

"It allows the kind of specialization that no one person is capable of, obviously," he says. "And here you've got a team where there is total mutual trust between them. Each is eager to assist the other in being fulfilled in a shared job. I'm absolutely sold on this kind of arrangement, given the right kind of people. They've both brought their problems to me and I think I'm better informed about what is going on in their department than I would have been with only one."

The couple differs in their perceptions of being assessed as a team. "I'm aware that I think my job security is very much dependent on him," Mary comments. "We're looked on as a couple, although we're doing different things. I think I got the job because of him, his background, and I don't like that, though I'm grateful for this first chance. I still have to deal with the side of me that doesn't want to work, but I enjoy the job and the contact with people. I don't think I would give it up."

Her husband feels that people are judging them together and so "if it's not working on one half, it's not going to work as a whole, though there is room for positive reactions to one person and negative to the other."

"Sharing," he feels, "is one of the things that I miss, personally in our society—the lack of community. We've gotten more involved to some degree. We've just made more of an effort. The specific job, as it is, I don't think would work very well if you just put two people in here. We really are a business manager, even though there are two of us, because we do collaborate."

Sharing the job has resulted in continuous readjustment in their family life.

"Our marriage has a wider scope to it," Mary says, "in that what we share is sort of a family project. I don't know if job sharing has made the marriage better, but dealing with Gordon's being unhappy and my being unhappy has."

Mary explains her feelings of being part of his work world: "I respect him, I always have, but when we go to a meeting and I see him do a good job, I feel really good about it. Before, I knew what

he did but I never could see it—see other people respond to him."
He not only has more time, she adds, but "feels better about
himself and has more energy to give to me."

"We have almost no time away from our children," she says,
"because we don't hire babysitters anymore. We can't afford it
and are not socializing as much. Our life is more relaxed. That has
to do with less money, too, I think."

Rearrangement of domestic responsibilities, since Gordon is no
longer working a 12-hour day, means that each parent shares
cooking, cleaning, and child care.

"It's driving me bananas," Gordon admits. "But as a basic
responsibility to get done, it's mine. I wanted to spend a lot more
time with the kids than I had before and that's been working out
pretty well. I can relate to them as people. It doesn't happen all the
time—most of the time, life is a little more than ordinary." But
it's satisfying and "we really get in touch with each other."

There is anxiety, he acknowledges, in shifting from fixed roles
at home. "From Mary's standpoint," he feels, "she has put a lot
of time and energy into accepting or finding ways of feeling good
about the roles as they are divided. This was more my initiative
than hers; so that caused some problems from her standpoint. She
actually has so much less free time."

New-found free time, for Gordon at least, is one of the hardest
things to cope with. "I completely underestimated," he explains,
"how difficult it would be to have time. One threat to it is
dissipating it, another is that it's very easy to get it filled up. It's
hard to preserve the space, very hard. And then also to make use
of it, because I've got to plan my day to use it well. It was O.K. for
awhile, because I just wanted to take it easy. It's delightful not
having to go in every day, but there was a way in which that was
satisfying because things were taken care of. The structure was
there, and the business environment. They had a lot of positive
things that I miss. I could go out to lunch whenever I wanted,
unlimited money from an expense account standpoint, within my
judgment. I got to travel pretty much as I wanted."

Both Gordon and Mary are tentative about their long term commitment to the change. Gordon feels that he has "opted out of a career," but adds that "nobody has to have a career."

"But it's hard," he says, "putting yourselves outside social expectations, social role models, though I don't think either one of us is particularly hung up on it now . . . doing what society expects of us."

They have agreed that they both want to maintain options—if Mary wishes to continue, or he to return to graduate school—still leaving open other ways to safeguard economic security. "One reason I went into business," Gordon says, "kind of came out of my own family background; I came from a poor family. And I really have a strong thing about not being dependent."

### Co-Directors of Personnel Development: One Entity

*Nora and John hold the position of co-directors of personnel development at a university. For the past five years they have been teaching, as well as developing and coordinating programs which serve 8,000 employees. They are responsible for supervising an office staff of ten.*

*They brought an impressive background when applying for the position, which was advertised as a one-person, full time directorship.*

*Both had strong experience and educational background, and together had developed a style of work ever since the time of their marriage. With graduate degrees in public health and administration, each had held jobs in related fields: John in positions at a hospital, in juvenile hall administration and probation, and as director of a state level program; Nora as a social case worker, private employment aide, and administrative officer in various governmental agencies. They had already shared a position as consultants to a state Department of Health, and the joint position of assistant visiting professor of human relations. After working together for some time, both earned doctoral degrees in human ecology.*

"It's a particular model," explains the vice president of the university. "It may be a singular model. I don't disentangle the way they work from the fact that there are two of them. I'd be surprised if you'd find a great many who could operate this way."

He explains that the fact that they had "pretty well developed their style" was an important consideration in the hiring. "Moreover, the directorship," he pointed out, "is not an ongoing operation in which there are day-to-day administrative demands that can be met only in a traditional structure and schedule."

Creation of the position had involved certain reorganization of the office so that it became responsible not only for earlier programs, like tuition assistance, but new employee orientation, courses on administrative practices, administrative development for mid-level managers on financial management, and organizational psychology. There was to be a clear mandate to increase the range of offerings for staff in order to provide career counseling to encourage staff in new jobs, thus creating an internal labor market within the institution. In terms of staff arrangements, the vice president explained, the university was open to changes which would increase flexibility, including part time tenure and revision of fringe benefits to allow for half time employment.

The interview process remains a vivid memory for John and Nora. Queried by some 16 staff, they responded by explaining the advantages to employers in terms of time, productivity, and creativity. "Two people—male and female," John remembers explaining, "could reach out better to larger numbers of staff."

Some members of the administration were skeptical about sharing a supervisory position, and several levels of personnel needed reassurance. John and Nora also remember the doubts of other married couples about their ability to work well together. They themselves, John explained, had become accustomed to the advantages. "Managers can get lonely." Both speak of the rewards of energy and support from each other.

The couple see themselves as one entity, and their method of using time reinforces this. Both are in the office in a continuous overlap. Originally their official hours each totalled 60 percent and were later extended to 70 percent, with equal pay checks and prorated benefits. Both see the job as more than 100 percent, they rarely take more than part of their vacation and, although they start mornings late at the office, they have already worked several hours at home.

"Both of us like the freedom to know that we can take the time we want," John explained. It also allows them to continue together their outside consulting and other part time teaching which they see reinforcing their primary job responsibilities.

"Basically, we work out our own hours," he adds, "but we prefer to be involved in all aspects of the job, being aware of what each is doing."

They are identical, in the vice president's view, with total responsibility for the office. "I might have said beforehand, how are they going to organize it? Each take a piece? But, if they divide it's not apparent to me." Both attend staff meetings. "If only one is there, it's a surprise," he says. "I make almost no adjustments; it's a matter of indifference which one I deal with. I know that what one tells me will represent a common position. There's a natural duality here; they may disagree, but I observe a small mutually supportive system between them, a great deal of respect for one another's opinions. Most people are not conscious of their individual strengths; they complement and reinforce each other."

Unlike the cases of some married couples sharing elsewhere, the university did not devise a contractual stipulation to cover the possibility of unequal performance. Although the vice president remembers his concern that the couple would become too much of a "package," he remarks that, "the only thing we've had is better appointment as co-directors. I have the feeling that we get more than our money's worth, this is not just a 70 percent contribution."

John and Nora are enthusiastic about their work and credit much of their success to the administrative support "giving us authority to do what we want to do and backing us up." They have increased the scope of their office, administering new programs and offering new courses which they teach jointly. Their careful, professional fashioning of new programs has substantially increased the mobility of staff within the institution, which was one important reason for the original office reorganization. "They've been very effective supervisors," the vice president says, "not only in their professional competence as teachers and organizers of programs within their office, but both are always there, and their particular style makes a difference in sharing as supervisors. They work very patiently at it and are very attentive to the individuals dependent on their organization, while still setting high standards."

"I think it's sort of a myth," John maintains, "that if you have two supervisors, people would play them off against each other. That's certainly a possibility, but if the two supervisors agree anyway, it doesn't make any difference. I think we have to be on our toes occasionally for people trying to play us off; you can kind of tell when that's happening."

"The biggest thing about our role as supervisors," Nora emphasizes, "is that because we're in organizational development, we have certain biases—namely, we believe in participatory management. It's partly because we believe in it and teach the concept that we made a decision early on that we'd try and implement that style here. We think it works better for job sharers than a more authoritarian style of leadership. In a sense, the management of this office is a shared function of the group, even though ultimately we're responsible if things fall apart. So most decision making that affects people here is done with a great deal of information from the group."

If there is any stress, for this couple, in working together, it is not surprisingly the need for time "to play."

"It's been hard," John says, "you know—the work is there to be done and it's easy to go home at night and do it and work until 11:00."

"Since the work is so interesting," Nora adds, "it's on our minds all the time. It's very, very difficult to say we'll take a night off or to take a weekend off completely. It's hard to stop."

The sharing is continued in domestic responsibilities, as well. "It's essential that the stuff at home is also shared," John remarks. "I learned early on, as a kid, when we all pitched in; it never bothered me, you know, that's not what boys do but girls do."

Nora adds, "It's sort of automatic by now. John does a lot more than I do in terms of housework."

Because they are so closely identified as a team, their sense of complete interdependence makes them recognize the need to be sensitive that they not appear too powerful a unit.

"I don't really think it affects the office," John feels. "I do think we have to be a little careful not to overpower people because there are two of us. You know, there is the united front kind of thing which is certainly more in the eyes of other people than it is in ours. We've had no problems particularly with it but there are a lot of people we know, because we are really close in many ways, who have a desire to look for some big flaw. It's in some ways a self-protective thing. I don't know if it may be envy, but it's kind of like 'see they do it and I know my wife and I couldn't do it.' When we run into people like that we try and say, 'look, there's nothing wrong with you, it's that with some people it works and some it doesn't.' Other people have perfectly fine marriages and work life and all of that and are not sharing a job. And I suspect from our experience we're relatively rare to work it out and continue to enjoy it."

They intend to continue sharing and apparently have no concerns about the future, although, as John observes, "it is unlikely that they would have a chance to become co-administrators at the next higher level."

"The only goal that I could conceive of in terms of organizational change as a team," Nora points out, "would be teaching elsewhere as well . . . putting more energy into teaching."

Both are thoughtful about criteria for successful sharing. Nora comments on the difficulty for those who are competitive or upwardly mobile.

"I think there are a lot of areas," she points out, "where they could get into competition with each other and get into political alliances for this kind of reason that would work to the detriment of the effort of the two."

"I would say that jobs that require a high degree of creativity would lend themselves to sharing," Nora continues, "with the proviso that a special kind of relationship could develop between two people. Compatibility, though important in any position, is twice as important in sharing. I'd say, myself, that a job that divides out neatly isn't necessarily the best job for sharing. It possibly would work, but not in terms of taking advantage of the added benefit of sharing, not like a job that's relatively unstructured and has room for development, change, and creativity."

"There is another way of looking at it, too," her husband interjects. "People who have a high tolerance for ambiguity, or fairly high, and jobs which have ambiguity in them lend themselves very well to job sharing. And I think that is one of the things that we can do that sometimes drives other people crazy. We can tolerate a lot more ambiguity than most people can."

As for advising any organization on hiring sharers, John emphasized: "For one thing, if people are going to share a job, I would really want to look at the people, in that they get excited by working together. In other words, is their product improved by the ideas and the interaction?"

# Chapter Five

# Looking Forward

The explicit aim of this study was to explore the desire for shared jobs, the different arrangements fashioned, and the personal outcomes to individuals. Survey data indicated a typology of sharers and sharing situations. Partnership profiles provided a sampling of individuals' motivations and reactions to the job sharing experience. The study was designed to emphasize employee responses, and sharers were allowed to speak for themselves, in large measure, in order to explore the effects of this new form of work on the individual rather than on the organization.

A number of policy implications emerge from the review of employee perceptions as they relate to organizational considerations. On the basis of this survey of job sharing experience, certain criteria for continued implementation can be suggested, and questions can be formulated for further examination in order to determine whether job sharing offers a valid employment pattern for the future.

*Employee Perceptions*

Although sharers primarily desired fewer hours at work, they generally sought those jobs in professional and occupational levels which they could not obtain on a part time, one-person basis. Partnership did provide a means to this end—the opportunity to work less time in positions normally unavailable except on a standard full time work schedule. Women, and men as well, were able to utilize education and training, maintain a sense of career continuity, or renew themselves in periods when skills and confidence might otherwise have atrophied. Job sharing in this sense related to different pressure periods in life—whether for start-up, training, re-entry, or slowing down of work and job time. The important concept of *balancing* of time and responsibilities implies particular periods of life for both younger as well as older workers.

But this alone did not distinguish sharers' arrangements from other part time work which carries some of the same advantages and is often characterized by similar satisfactions of higher morale and greater energy. The combination of fewer hours together with the added benefits of partnering—the sense of choice and autonomy in terms of task and time—is what differentiated job sharing for many employees. Whenever this combination existed, sharers valued the results of greater flexibility, increased opportunity for learning, and the sense of a worthwhile and complete job. They found advantages in the cooperation and support in those positions designed as less interdependent as well as in the more collaborative teaming that enhanced their sense of accomplishment and effectiveness.

On the other side, there are real problems for the individual sharer. Some are difficulties which arise because of the presence of two employees rather than one. Others are those exacerbated by joint rather than single responsibility and therefore vary with particular personal partner relationships. If part time work is difficult to arrange and maintain, job sharing may be even more so.

Beyond the problem of confining time to allocated hours, sharing raises concerns about maintaining equal time. To the question of appropriate salary and fringe benefits, it adds the complication of equitable division between partners. Furthermore, since arrangements generally have been singular or few within most organizations, the sharer is often left unsure whether job tenure depends on team or individual evaluation. This has often provided added incentive to perform, a familiar "Hawthorne" effect, but it has also inhibited discussion and resolution of potential problems between the pair or between the pair and supervisor. Finally, even when sharers apparently accept the slower accrual rate of time toward salary advancement, they may worry about the likelihood of promotion to higher grade levels.

As for the personal element of partner relationships, sharing in collaborative arrangements often proved the most exhilarating but the most challenging. Some individuals or pairs turned to advantage the ambiguity of job requirements and of jurisdiction, but others found the demands too frustrating for productive performance. Perceptions of competition and cooperation vary greatly. What appears to be loss of individual identity within one partnership may be sensed as positive team image in another. In some situations, when one partner was apparently stronger in his or her abilities, the value for the individual of complementary teaming was lost.

Although the evidence of this study indicates that most job sharers perceive their experiences as positive and successful, obviously the weighing of advantages and disadvantages must rest with each individual. Indeed, a re-examination at later periods of these same sharers' judgments would undoubtedly show attitude changes. For potential sharers, this judgment will remain a theoretical question unless they are permitted the opportunity to make the choice.

## Organizational Reasons for Hiring

With the exception of certain small scale experiments, only a few job sharing arrangements were initiated by organizations which had predetermined what positions were to be opened to sharing. In some others, management perceived as suitable those jobs that were already part time, one-person, and found it not inconvenient to have two employees. *Most arrangements, however, were initiated by workers, made possible because the organization responded to their needs and considered innovation potentially rewarding in instances when particular applicants presented themselves.* This held true even when organizational policy for sharing already existed, because supervisor's approval in each instance was a necessary pre-condition for hiring.

A combination of specific factors facilitated the initiation of sharing arrangements. Organizations were more likely to permit sharing when one or, more often, both applicants were already in its employ. Whether or not prospective sharers were known to them, supervisors often added a further prerequisite—judgment that both members of the pair would otherwise be capable of covering the job alone. In at least a few situations (particularly teachers), the advantage of a pair as "role models" offered an added incentive. In other cases, the presence of other part time personnel undoubtedly favored the introduction of job sharing arrangements. Management was also intrigued by the potential advantage of having two employees to meet time pressure jobs, pressure over long or short periods. In many instances, the organization anticipated that a pair would bring a greater variety of expertise through the combining of complementary skills. Particularly in positions requiring coordination and liaison, management envisaged that two sharers would be better able than one full time employee to respond to a larger number of staff or clients. This potential advantage of sharing had heretofore not been particularly recognized.

All of these conditions also applied generally when management actively recruited or made known its amenability to sharing in large numbers. But here other purposes motivated decisions, including the desire to: 1) increase affirmative action hirings in both entry and higher level positions; 2) make more attractive those positions prone to high turnover rates; and 3) allow, in those occupations with more defined tenure systems such as teaching, new entrants while still retaining older personnel who might wish to reduce work hours. This last factor merits special emphasis because it implied *the potential of sharing as a cost saver.* Although not a primary motivation in the early years, nor fully assessed as yet, school administrators were among the first to recognize that (dependent on methods of fringe benefit provision) the pairing of personnel made possible the combination of lower and higher ends of the salary scale.

## Considerations in Instituting Job Sharing

Limited experience with job sharing on a large scale within single organizations makes cost-benefit analysis premature. It does indicate that successful initiation will be based on organizational ability to establish policy on the following considerations—all of which carry a commitment for careful pre-planning:

1) Eligibility rules and recruitment procedures need to be examined to permit the widest possible applicant pool at several job levels. Management will have to consider ways of determining the optimum number of part timers and job sharers in proportion to its total staff. It will want to decide whether sharing shall be available only to current employees or also to outside applicants. If sharing is limited to those already within the organization, then how important a factor is seniority? Whether or not new hires are allowed, and this would seem highly desirable, all efforts should be made to prevent involuntary sharing. Some organizations have suggested maintaining separate part time only applicant lists, whereas others have accepted applications from both single full time candidates and two sharers for the same position.

A key factor in the decision process is the support of union representatives, where applicable, and of other staff, especially immediate supervisors. This presupposes advance discussion of both advantages and complications of sharing.

2) Job sharing requires more attention to job descriptions. Obviously, the organization will find it less complicated to plan for two employees when time and tasks are clearly delineated and easily divisible. The difficulty arises with more creative or open-ended jobs when the jurisdiction for deciding job content and responsibility is left unclear. To avoid the tendency to depend on sharers alone, distinction needs to be drawn between areas open for partnership decision and those circumscribed by the organization.

3) In the interview process, again depending on how much collaboration appears to be called for, it will be desirable to leave flexible the method of matching partners. Firms that insist that hiring be dependent on the appearance of applicants in ready made pairs, may find this impossible to ensure. This does not preclude, however, the desirability of allowing partners a degree of choice in team composition.

4) Because the sense of a whole or "real" job compared with one considered temporary or "spot" is paramount, organizations need to realize that entitlement to and equitable allocation of fringe benefits are crucial. This differs from salary division, where differentials are more likely to be considered legitimate recognition of experience and training levels. Experience has shown that outside of per capita costs, prorating of those other benefits which are proportionate to salary can be workable.

5) Organizations will need to consider whether performance reviews are appropriate in terms of each partner, for the team as a unit, or in some cases on both levels. Because there are so many variations within sharing positions and the relationships are dynamic rather than static, the most important factor will be provision for periodic consultation with teams to assess progress and problems. Implied here is the likelihood of stress, particularly in early stages of sharing arrangements, when new and different arrangements are introduced alongside the accepted norm.

6) The difficult matters of promotion and reversibility relate more properly to the unsettled questions of the future extension of job sharing, but should be noted here because they must be considered when the organization considers policy initiatives. Experience indicates that management has only rarely determined whether positions are limited to the tenure of particular individuals or whether it will leave open the possibility of hiring another half and/or pair, should one partner or both leave the position. The advantage to the organization when an incumbent trains a new sharer has been

discussed earlier. The long range negative effect, i.e., the sharers' concern over promotion uncertainty, has not yet been tested owing to the relatively short term of most experiences. Only in rare instances have sharers retained the same status when moving to higher level positions within the same organization.

Similarly, few organizations have clear-cut policies on reversibility—the return to full time jobs relinquished by the same individual in order to share. Some (among them, school districts) have guaranteed sharers the opportunity to return to full time status on demand. Others (some county offices) require sharers to return to full time when one half leaves and eligibility requirements preclude the hiring of another half. Still other organizations have left open the question for later review.

## Unsettled Questions

Before predictions can be ventured as to whether job sharing will become more widespread, some major questions still remain to be explored. Before raising them, however, a more fundamental issue must be examined—whether recognition of the option's value depends on its usage by large numbers over a fixed period of time.

Although it is assumed that individual partnerships will continue and others be instituted more easily as knowledge of examples spreads, this still implies that the arrangement is for the singular few who are most able to persist in pioneering. But, if job sharing is to become an accepted employment option for larger numbers, there will need to be more varied opportunities across a *spread of levels and occupations.*

This does not mean that the option needs to be justified by great numbers to prove itself. In fact, it is doubtful that a large proportion of the labor force *at a given time* will want or be able to work for half salary, especially in situations with the unknowns inherent in many partnership arrangements. Perhaps the greatest value of job sharing will be its capacity to *afford choices at different periods in the individual's work lifetime.* Will the concept be considered worthy of continued experimentation despite the varying tenure of individual job sharers? Much depends on the future perception of jobs and their match to people's needs.

A first question often posed is: *What kinds of jobs can be shared?* Many more than have already been instituted, judging by previous examples. Certainly some positions appear more amenable than others to division in task and time. Jobs of the future will be found in service and clerical occupations and in the professions more than in industry. The first two have already lent themselves to sharing of the less interdependent, i.e., "split," type. Although all too often these are repetitive and routine jobs, their restructuring does improve the match between individual preferences and/or peak efficiency periods with time on the job. Furthermore, in some of these arrangements partners have valued cooperation and support as a mitigating factor. Perhaps a palliative rather than a panacea, sharing, as differentiated from part time, may still allow more task choices and to this extent improved job content.

More important, higher level positions—those commanding better salaries, either supervisory, liaison, or "creative"—are not usually perceived as applicable to joint responsibility. Yet many have lent themselves to successful sharing. As described earlier, these may be more difficult to organize and to maintain because consistent performance depends on the delicate balance of personal and organizational factors. In the long run, the test of sharing depends on an ability to envisage and experiment with these jobs.

The appropriate matching of partners will remain an important consideration. Much depends on the right combination of skills, sharers' sense of compatibility, trust and positive competition, and on their ability to communicate well. But the partner relationship, while crucial, does not hold the sole key to success. In such arrangements, much is demanded from the organization to provide a favorable environment. Management will need to take into account the dynamic nature of job content and partner relationships and to examine its own conception of authority in order to allow sharers room to accommodate to each other and to the organization. Successful sharing between two employees also connotes a pervasive spirit of cooperation and, indeed, of participation by other employees as well. In this connection, one can only surmise the possible long range effects of job sharers on other employees in the organization—an intriguing area for further study.

Instead of job requirements alone, the question might be amended to add: *What kinds of people might wish to share jobs if the opportunities were available?* Discussion of alternative work patterns often elicits the charge that sharers, like others seeking change, are special people for whom work is a calling rather than an economic necessity. Experience does show that organizations have been willing to innovate when pressed by the most informed and articulate—those who are also the most able to afford the risks now characteristic of job sharing.

An inventory of the potential labor supply suggested by the demographic, cultural and economic changes outlined in Chapter I would show that the labor force is becoming more heterogeneous. These trends included: the continued demand for labor market entry by women; family changes resulting from a higher percentage of working parents; the competition for jobs by a more educated population with heightened expectations of work; and the new examination of a once rigid retirement age by an increasing older population. Such a changing labor force may well stimulate innovation in recruitment and scheduling. For example, particular attention needs to be paid to the applicability of job sharing arrangements to those at different stages of employment development, i.e., the pairing of younger workers with older trained personnel in an apprenticeship type of system as well as older workers in teams.

Still another unresolved question centers on the *likelihood of sharing in large organizations with relatively rigid personnel policies.* The assumption might be made that management in these firms will find it even more difficult to institute change. At the same time, public sector organizations in education and government, particularly, have shown the most inclination to consider job sharing at levels not hitherto open to part time.

It now appears that events of the past year, gathering momentum during the writing of this study, will provide further stimulus. Whether or not the taxpayers revolt takes the form of California's Proposition 13, the cost of public service throughout the U.S. is already under increasing scrutiny. Local, city, and state governments will be pressed to examine ways to cut costs and to make difficult judgments on maintenance of services.

It is important to point out that the impetus which led to development of the greatest number of shared jobs (as split codes) during the past years came about because a variety of options were developed by union negotiations with organizations. Management was most likely to offer and implement job sharing in conjunction with other time reducing measures. Such combinations, which also included options of varying percentage bases, existed in examples at the state and county levels in California. Furthermore, when reductions in the work force were threatened, employees whose jobs were not at issue were among those who preferred to reduce hours through job sharing as well.[1]

Government as employer is already beginning to provide some models. Its capacity to meet problems of costs, eligibility, recruitment, and regulations on retirement may be applicable in some measure to private firms who have evinced less interest so far in job sharing.

The *role of unions* poses another unknown. Organized labor's opposition to less than full time work may be changing, but it remains to be seen whether unions become a positive force for change toward alternative work patterns. What can be said is that the negative impact of unions appears to be lessening. Although some officers still object publicly to the potential loss of full time

---

1. In this connection, we might note that recent discussion of reduced time measures involves the provision of short time compensation for both public and private employers. It presupposes the desire for reduced time, even though its voluntary nature has yet to be tested to determine whether it depends on decisions by the individual, by groups, or by union/employee representatives.

jobs, certain locals of government employees (S.E.I.U.), when pressed by their membership, have actively negotiated to include job sharing. At the same time, somewhat less is heard of the traditional union stance that part time work is generally involuntary and offers second class employment because of limited fringe benefits and career opportunities. A group of labor representatives who examined European alternative work schedules reported that, compared with traditional permanent part time work, a shared job offered the advantages that its content "which is in fact a full-time job, is more likely to be of higher quality and the pay is likely to be better."[2]

Future examination of job sharing will also turn to the questions involved in *limiting actual dollar costs, in terms of proportionate numbers of sharers and their length of job tenure.* Much more cost information needs to be developed before either private or public organizations are likely to consider larger scale implementation measures. Added to such important inhibitors as the inconvenience of change and complications of the option, job sharing is likely to increase dollar costs before its advantages can be judged by management. Beyond those costs incurred for initial training and overhead are the mandatory per capita fringe benefit costs. The per capita cost of Social Security and Unemployment Insurance may be perceived as a real drawback to opening opportunities at higher salary levels. Other fringe benefits, such as health insurance, when not omitted entirely for sharers, have been allotted for convenience or for equity on the same basis as for full time work, and as such have proved expensive. Many organizations have found prorated systems economically feasible. On the other hand, it is apparent that the "market basket" approach of customizing each arrangement to suit the needs of individual employees has also thwarted large scale experimentation within the organization.

---

2. *Innovations in Working Patterns: Report of the U.S. Trade Union Seminar on Alternative Work Patterns in Europe,* prepared by Jeffrey M. Miller and published jointly by The Communications Workers of America and The German Marshall Fund of the U.S. Washington, D.C.: May 1978, p. 18.

NEEDS FOR THE FUTURE

The leadership to promote job sharing, and with it the examination of these questions, has rested until recently with women's employment groups allied informally with other agencies and groups concerned with alternative work patterns and quality of work life issues. They have articulated the advantages of job sharing to the organization: better use of skills, increased supply of qualified personnel, lower rates of absenteeism and sick leave, and increased productivity through greater employee morale and energy.[3] The higher incidence of job sharing initiatives in particular geographic areas often reflects the efforts of these groups. Their role, therefore, will remain important, not only in generating more widespread awareness of the option, but in actively assisting potential job sharers and facilitating changes within interested organizations. There is also a need for additional small scale demonstration projects in both the private and public sector to provide data for a more systematic analysis and to disseminate information more widely.

Congress has recently enacted legislation increasing part time and job sharing for federal workers and action on the executive directive to the Civil Service Commission is under way. Other information is expected from the federally supported program in Wisconsin. Proposed research on work sharing, requested by the Department of Labor, may bear on job sharing. Beyond the investigating of inhibiting legislation is the question of the desirability of continuing and/or amending the legislation which provides incentives through tax credits, for example, to stimulate innovation by private employers.

But, if future investigation takes the form of cost-benefit analysis, it will still have limited value because the choices involved in implementing new work arrangements will not rest on these

---

3. Only a few studies on alternative work patterns have addressed the organizational point of view. See Stanley D. Nollen, *et al.*, *Permanent Part-Time Employment: The Manager's Perspective* (New York: Praeger Publishers, 1978), and Allan R. Cohen and Herman Gadon, *Alternative Work Schedules: Integrating Individual and Organizational Needs* (Reading, MA: Addison-Wesley, 1978).

answers alone. Beyond the narrow cost-benefit calculations, a larger conceptual framework should give due weight to more important underlying attitudes on time, jobs, and work. Such a fundamental rethinking would question the artificiality of the time dimension in many jobs when the job, rather than the work itself, is measured as full time. It would ask how work expands or contracts with the time allotted or paid for. Even more important, it would consider the relation of work to the totality of life, daily and over the years. If changes in jobs and careers at different stages of life are becoming more usual, is it any less reasonable to recognize the legitimacy of variations in time at work?

Job sharing will be relevant whenever it calls attention to the need for choices at different stages and when it is properly considered among other forms of work flexibility, particularly those concerned with deviation from the standard work week and work year. We only have to reflect on the fact that the standard work patterns have not always been standard, but have evolved historically to meet changing needs. Reductions in time through sabbatical leave, as well as through weekly and yearly percentages, are now being explored. Further, new views on the relation of education to work and on the meaning of continuing education will bring wider scope to the discussion of all alternatives. Job sharing takes its place among these innovative arrangements as one of the various ways to meet the needs of the future, as well as current, labor force.

> The central problem of industrial relations around the world is not capital versus labor, but rather the structuring of the labor force—how it gets recruited, developed, and maintained. This is the daily business of industrial relations everywhere.[4]

---

4. Clark Kerr, *et al., Industrialism and Industrial Man* (Middlesex, England: Pelican Press, 1973), pp. 280-281.

SELECTED READINGS
JOB SHARING

Bagchi, Pat. "Job Sharing." *Peninsula Magazine,* April 1976, pp. 74-76.

Bergmann, Martha. "Job Sharing." *Bootlegger,* March-June 1974, pp. 44-46.

Catalyst, Inc. *Profiles of Individuals.* New York: Catalyst, 1973.

Coote, Chris. "Staying Whole as Halves." *New Physicians,* February 1977, pp. 35, 36.

Dubrofsky, Lynn. "Job Sharing." In *Working Couples,* edited by Rhona N. and Robert Rapoport. New York: Harper & Row/Rutledge, 1978.

Gallese, Liz Roman. "Two for the Price of One: Colleges Say They Get More for Their Money by Hiring a Couple to Share One Faculty Job." *The Wall Street Journal,* April 19, 1974.

Gronseth, Eric. "Work Sharing Families: Adaptations of Pioneering Families with Husband and Wife in Part-Time Employment." *Acta Sociologica,* Vol. 18, No. 2-3, pp. 202-221.

Hoffman, Lenore and DeSole, Gloria. *Careers and Couples: An Academic Question.* New York: Modern Language Association of America, Commission on the Status of Women in the Profession, 1976.

"Job Sharing Catches On." *Business Week,* October 25, 1976, p. 112E.

"Job Sharing for Teachers Catches On." *Nation's Schools Report.* McGraw-Hill, Inc., March 29, 1976, pp. 1, 2.

"Job Sharing in the Schools." *Public Personnel Administration: Policies and Practices for Personnel.* Report No. 9, Prentice-Hall, Inc., November 3, 1976.

"Joys of Sharing." *Human Behavior,* November 1976, p. 36.

Knickerbocker, Brad. "Job Sharing Catches On." *Christian Science Monitor,* December 13, 1976, p. 2.

_____ . "Government Moves to Hire More Part-Time Employees." *Christian Science Monitor,* March 8, 1978, p. 6.

Lazer, Robert I. "Job Sharing as a Pattern of Permanent Part-Time Work." *The Conference Board Record,* October 1975, pp. 57-61.

Meier, Gretl and Barney Olmsted. *A Beginning Dialogue: Relevance of the American Experience with Job Sharing to European Employment Issues.* Grant report to the German Marshall Fund. Palo Alto, CA: New Ways to Work, 1978.

Meier, Gretl, *et al. Job-Sharing in the Schools.* Palo Alto, CA: New Ways to Work, 1976.

_____ . "Shared Job Project in California Stimulates Labor and Management Interest." *World of Work Report,* Work in America Institute, September 1976, p. 7.

New Ways to Work. *Bibliography on Job Sharing.* Palo Alto, CA: New Ways to Work, revised 1979.

_____ . *A Booklet of General Information About Job Sharing.* Palo Alto, CA: New Ways to Work, June 1977.

_____ . "Job Sharing Project Final Report." Report of 1975-76 CETA-Funded Pilot Project. Palo Alto, CA: New Ways to Work, January 1977.

_____ . *Working Less But Enjoying It More: A Guide to Splitting or Sharing Your Job.* Palo Alto, CA: New Ways to Work, 1978.

Olmsted, Barney. "Job Sharing: A New Way to Work." *Personnel Journal,* February 1977, pp. 78-81.

_____ . "Job Sharing: A New Way to Work." *Women's Agenda,* May 1976, pp. 3-4.

"One Answer to Hard-to-Fill Jobs: Let Two People Share the Work." *ALERT,* New York Research Institute of America, April 20, 1977.

Reynolds, Anne and King, C. "Why Not Partnership Librarians?" *Bay State Librarian,* February 1969, pp. 3-4.

Sandler, Rhoda and Platt, Judith. "Job Sharing in Montgomery County." *Library Journal,* November 1, 1973, pp. 3234-5.

Sawyer, Kathy. "Job-Sharing: Growing Trend." *Washington Post,* December 26, 1977.

Special Libraries Association. *News Bulletin* of the Boston Chapter, May-June 1976, pp. 45-49, 55-59. Includes Hughes, S.D. "Job Sharing: The Idea and The Practice," Howell, Jane L. "Job Sharing for Librarians," Laursen, Irene and Rouse, Diana. "Job Sharing in the Wellesley College Science Library: A Preliminary Report,"

Anderson, Ann M. "Job Sharing at the Winchester Public Library," and Laursen, Irene. "Alternative Work Patterns: A Selective Bibliography."

Terrebonne, Bob and Terrebonne, Nancy. "Sharing An Academic Appointment." Paper delivered at the Popular Culture Association Convention, Chicago, April 23, 1976.

"The Two-Professor Family: A Trend That May Be Difficult To Continue." *Campus Report,* Stanford University, May 25, 1977.

"Two Employees for the Price of One." *Personal Report for the Executive.* The Research Institute of America, Inc., April 12, 1977.

"Two for the Price of One." *Time,* May 3, 1976, p. 68.

## RELATED READINGS

*Alternatives in the World of Work.* Washington, D.C.: Committee on Alternative Work Patterns and National Center for Productivity and Quality of Working Life, 1976.

Anschell, Susie. *A Place for Part-Timers in Your Organization.* Seattle: University of Washington, Institute of Government Research, January 1978.

Baker, Helen and Friedman, Rita B. *The Use of Part-Time Workers in the War Effort.* Princeton, NJ: Princeton University, Industrial Relations Section, June 1943.

Bengtsson, Jarl. "Recurrent Education: Progress and Pitfalls." *OECD Observer,* September 1978, pp. 12-15.

Best, Fred, ed. *The Future of Work.* Englewood Cliffs, NJ: Prentice-Hall, 1973.

Brozan, Nadine. "Part-Time Workers—Making Inroads Into a Full-Time World." *New York Times,* October 16, 1973.

Burkett, Gary L. and Gabrielson, Ira W. "A Study of the Demand for Part Time Residency Programs." *Journal of Medical Education,* October 1976, pp. 829-834.

Civil Service Commission. "Legal Limitations on Flexible and Compressed Work Schedules for Federal Employees." Report to Congress by the Controller General of the U.S., October 21, 1974.

Crittenden, Ann. "Women Work and Men Change." *New York Times,* January 9, 1977, p. 22.

de Grazia, Sebastian. *Of Time, Work and Leisure.* New York: Anchor Books, 1964.

Dickson, Paul. *The Future of the Work Place.* New York: Weybright and Talley, 1975.

Dullea, Georgia. "Vast Changes in Society Traced to the Rise of Working Women." *New York Times,* November 29, 1977, pp. 1, 28.

*Equality of Opportunity and Treatment for Women Workers.* Report VIII. Geneva: International Labor Office, 1975.

Evans, Archibald A. *Flexibility in Working Life: Opportunities for Individual Choice.* Paris: Organization for Economic Cooperation and Development, 1973.

Eyde, Lorraine. *Flexibility Through Part-Time Employment of Career Women in the Public Service.* U.S. Civil Service Commission Professional Series 75-3, June 1975.

Flexible Careers. *A Report from Flexible Careers.* Chicago: Flexible Careers, November 1974.

Ginsberg, Eli. "Work Structuring and Manpower Realities." In *The Quality of Working Life,* Vol. I. Edited by Louis E. Davis and Albert B. Cherns. New York: The Free Press, 1967, pp. 368-377.

Glickman, Albert S. and Brown, Zenia H. *Changing Schedules of Work: Patterns and Implications.* Kalamazoo, MI: The W. E. Upjohn Institute for Employment Research, 1974.

"Good Jobs Go Part-Time." *Money,* October 1977, pp. 80-86.

Graham, Benjamin. *The Flexible Work Year: An Answer to Unemployment.* Santa Barbara, CA: Center for the Study of Democratic Institutions, 1964.

Greenwald, Carol S. and Liss, Judith. "Part Time Workers Can Bring Higher Productivity." *Harvard Business Review,* September 1973, p. 6.

"Half Year Stint Gives His Job More Zest." *Washington Post,* December 25, 1977.

Haller, Willi. "Flexiyear: One Ultimate Unit Hour Concept." Paper prepared for InterFlex, New York, 1977.

Hedges, Janice Neipert. "New Patterns for Working Time." *Monthly Labor Review,* February 1973, pp. 3-8.

_____ . "How Many Days Make a Work Week?" *Monthly Labor Review,* April 1975, pp. 29-36.

Institute of Governmental Affairs, University of Wisconsin. "Survey of the Attitudes of City of Madison Employees Toward Alternative Work Patterns." Final Report, May 1977.

International Labor Office. *Making Work More Human: Working Conditions and Environment.* Report of the Director General, Geneva, 1975.

Janjic, Marion. "Part Time Work in Public Service." *International Labor Review,* April 1972.

Kahne, Hilda. "Future Issues For and About Women: An Economist's View." Paper presented to the Lilly Endowment, Inc., Indianapolis, 1976 (unpublished).

Kreps, Juanita M. and Leaper, R. John. "Home Work, Market Work and the Allocations of Time." In *Women and the American Economy.* Englewood Cliffs, NJ: Prentice-Hall, 1976.

Kronholz, June. "Management Practices Change to Reflect Role of Women Employees." *Wall Street Journal,* September 13, 1978.

Leed, B. Jean, ed. *Part Time Careers in Seattle.* Seattle: Focus on Part Time Careers, Inc., 1976.

Levitan, Sar A. *Reducing Worktime as a Means to Combat Unemployment.* Kalamazoo, MI: The W. E. Upjohn Institute for Employment Research, 1964.

Maric, D. *Adapting Working Hours to Modern Needs.* Geneva: International Labor Office, 1977.

McCarthy, Maureen E. *The Extent of Alternative Work Schedules in State Government.* Washington, D.C.: National Council for Alternative Work Patterns, 1977.

National Council for Alternative Work Patterns. *Alternative Work Schedule Directory: First Edition.* Washington, D.C.: National Council for Alternative Work Patterns, 1978.

_____. *National Conference on Alternative Work Schedules Resource Packet.* Washington, D.C.: National Council for Alternative Work Patterns, 1977.

Nordheimer, Jan. "The Family in Transition: A Challenge From Within." *New York Times,* November 27, 1977, p. 1.

Organization for Economic Cooperation and Development. *Lifelong Allocations of Time.* Report prepared by J. deChalendar, Paris, 1976.

_____. *New Patterns for Working Time.* Final report and supplement to final report of International Conference, Paris, 1973.

_____. *Policies for Life at Work.* Report prepared by the Joint Working Party on Internal Industrial Environment, with *Annex: Towards a Policy for Life at Work* by Kenneth Walker and Richard Shore, Paris, 1977.

"Part Time Employment." *OECD Observer,* June 1968.

"Part Time Employment: A Manager's Alternative in Staffing." Department of Health, Education, and Welfare, Federal Women's Program, May 1973.

"Part Time Jobs Appeal to Growing Number of Workers." *Washington Post,* December 28, 1977.

Pingree, Suzanne and Butler, Matilda. "Nepotism's Ghost: Attitudes Toward Hiring Wives and Husbands in Academic Departments." Paper prepared for annual convention of the Association for Education in Journalism, San Diego, August 1974.

Porter, Sylvia. "Flexitime Concept Gaining Favor." *San Francisco Chronicle,* June 4, 1976, p. 62.

Price, Charlton. *Alternatives in the World of Work.* Conference report, National Commission on Productivity and Quality of Working Life, Washington, D.C., 1976.

Prywes, Ruth W. *Study on the Development of a Non-Standard Work Day or Work Week for Women.* Springfield, VA: National Technical Information Service, 1974.

Quindlen, Anna. "Self-Fulfillment: Independence vs. Intimacy." *New York Times,* November 28, 1977, p. 1.

Rehn, Gösta. "For Greater Flexibility of Working Life." *OECD Observer,* February 1973, pp. 3-7.

Rosow, Jerome M., ed. *The Worker and The Job.* Englewood Cliffs, NJ: Prentice-Hall, Inc., 1974.

Sawyer, Kathy. "Keeping Up with the Joneses Beginning to Lose Its Appeal." *Washington Post,* December 25, 1977.

_____ . "Tailoring Schedules to Suit Workers." *Washington Post,* December 27, 1977.

_____ . "Unpaid Time-Off Studied." *Washington Post,* December 28, 1977.

Schwartz, Felice. "Converging Work Roles of Men and Women." *Business and Society Review/Innovation* 7, Autumn 1973.

_____ . "New Work Patterns: For Better Use of Womanpower." *Management Review,* May 1974.

Seashore, Stanley E. "Assessing the Quality of Working Life: The U.S. Experience." *Labor and Society,* April 1976, pp. 67-79.

_____ . "Defining and Measuring the Quality of Working Life." In *The Quality of Working Life,* Vol. I. Edited by Louis E. Davis and Albert B. Cherns. New York: The Free Press, 1976, pp. 105-118.

Teriet, Bernhard. "Flexiyear Schedules—Only A Matter of Time?" *Monthly Labor Review,* December 1977, pp. 62-65.

Terkel, Studs. *Working.* New York: Pantheon Books, 1972.

Wirtz, Willard and the National Manpower Institute. *The Boundless Resource.* Washington, D.C.: The New Republic Book Co., 1975.

# APPENDIX

SURVEY FOR

## "AN APPRAISAL FOR JOB SHARING IN THE U.S."

### PART I - THE JOB

**1. Is your job:** (236)

a. ☐ a full-time position shared with one other person?
☐ a full-time position shared with two or more?
☐ more than a full-time position shared with one or more persons? (e.g., 1½ positions, 3 persons)

b. **Are you still employed in this position?** (215)

☐ yes          ☐ no

**2. Do you consider your job:** (231)

☐ shared          ☐ split

**3. What is your area of work?** (238)

a. ☐ education          ☐ counseling, social work          ☐ library          ☐ research
☐ administration          ☐ clerical, secretarial          ☐ medical          ☐ other: _____

b. **What is your title?** (238) _____

**4. What is the composition of your team?** (238)

☐ male/male    ☐ male/female    ☐ female/female

**a. Are you and your partner related?** (235)

☐ no    ☐ yes - If yes, how? _____

**b. Did you know each other before working in this position?** (237)

☐ yes    ☐ no

**5. How was this job structured before?** (236)

a. ☐ newly created job    ☐ full-time, one person    ☐ shared position, two persons
                          ☐ part-time, one person    ☐ shared position, three or more persons

**b. Did you previously hold this position full-time?** (230)

☐ yes    ☐ no

**6. How long have you held this position with a partner?** (237)

☐ less than      ☐ 1 - 3 years      ☐ more than 5 years
  6 months
☐ 7 - 12 months  ☐ 4 - 5 years

**7. When seeking this position, were you:** (234)

a. employed?
- ☐ less than 1 year
- ☐ 1 - 3 years
- ☐ more than 3 years

b. unemployed?
- ☐ less than 3 months
- ☐ 3 months - 1 year
- ☐ more than 1 year

**8. If previously employed, your last job was:** (215)

- ☐ full-time
- ☐ part-time
- ☐ shared job
- ☐ other: _____

**9. Why did you leave your last job?** *(Please number all relevant items in both columns in order of their importance to you.)*

a. because you wanted a: (140)
- ____ more challenging job
- ____ higher salary
- ____ change in geographical location
- ____ change in nature of organization
- ____ other: _____

b. because you preferred a: (108)
- ____ full-time position
- ____ part-time job
- ____ shared job
- ____ other: _____

c. ☐ because job terminated (238)

**10. Who initiated your job?** (232)

- ☐ yourself
- ☐ your partner
- ☐ union
- ☐ employing organization
- ☐ agency (employment, counseling)
- ☐ other: _____

**11. Were there any unusual difficulties in creating this job?** (214)

    ☐ no

    ☐ yes, because: *(please list all relevant items in order of importance)*
          (128 mentions)

        \_\_\_\_\_ salary level (total)
        \_\_\_\_\_ salary division (between partners)
        \_\_\_\_\_ provision of benefits
        \_\_\_\_\_ pro-rating of benefits
        \_\_\_\_\_ finding a partner
        \_\_\_\_\_ keeping a partner
        \_\_\_\_\_ organizational personnel policy
        \_\_\_\_\_ other: _____

**12. Did you have any special counseling about job sharing?** (236)

    ☐ yes    ☐ no

**13. Why did you feel this job was suitable for sharing?** *(Please number all relevant items in order of their importance to you.)* (349 mentions)

    \_\_\_\_\_ variety of skills needed    \_\_\_\_\_ need for overlap time
    \_\_\_\_\_ tedious    \_\_\_\_\_ high pressure
    \_\_\_\_\_ detailed    \_\_\_\_\_ other: _____
    \_\_\_\_\_ challenging opportunity for collaboration

**14. Were you hired together?** (233)

    ☐ yes    ☐ no

**15. If not hired at the same time:**

  a. **Did the first person train the other?** (158)

      ☐ yes      ☐ no

  b. **Were you trained** (159)

      ☐ together      ☐ separately      ☐ not trained at all

**16. What is the total salary range of the position?** (230)

  a. ☐ below $8,500      ☐ $8,501 - $16,500      ☐ $16,501 - $25,000      ☐ above $25,000

  b. **Do both partners receive equal pay?** (217)

      ☐ yes      ☐ no

**17. Have you received a salary increase?** (228)

      ☐ cost of living      ☐ merit      ☐ both      ☐ neither

**18. Your entitlement to fringe benefits is:** (228)

  ☐ same coverage as full-time employees in your organization
  ☐ same coverage as full-time employees, but through a pro-rated arrangement
  ☐ no fringe benefits
  ☐ other: _____

178

19. **Does this job involve public contact?** (237)

☐ heavy   ☐ moderate   ☐ little or none

20. **Do you supervise others in the organization?** (237)

☐ no   ☐ 1 - 5   ☐ 6 - 10   ☐ 11 or more

# PART II - THE ORGANIZATION

21. **Is your organization:** (237)

☐ service oriented   ☐ product oriented

22. **Is your organization:** (236)

☐ private - nonprofit   ☐ public - government
☐ private - profit   ☐ public - education
   ☐ other: _____

23. **Approximately how many employees are in your organization (for teachers: district)?** (224)

☐ 1 - 25   ☐ 1,001 - 5,000
☐ 26 - 100   ☐ 5,001 - 10,000
☐ 101 - 500   ☐ more than 10,000
☐ 501 - 1,000

**24. Are there other sharing teams in your organization or department (district or school)?** (215)

☐ none
☐ less than 5

☐ between 6 and 10
☐ more than 10

**25. Is your organization unionized?** (230)

☐ yes          ☐ no

**Are you a union member?** (229)

☐ yes          ☐ no

## PART III - THE SHARING RELATIONSHIP

**26. Are your partner's skills:** (234)

☐ complementary to yours
☐ the same as yours
☐ different but complementary

☐ different and not complementary
please explain: _____

_____

**27. Is your work primarily divided by:** (233)

☐ time          ☐ tasks

**28. How is work time arranged between you and your partner?** (225)

☐ half-days
☐ split weeks
☐ week-on, week-off

☐ all time overlap
☐ no fixed schedule
☐ other: _____

29. **Was this arrangement based on:** (232)

☐ a choice made by you and your partner
☐ organizational constraints
☐ specific task requirement (public contact, space, etc.)
☐ other: _____

30. **Do you feel that there have been changes in partner relationship since your job started?** (231)

a. ☐ no changes
☐ yes, toward more collaboration
☐ yes, toward more separation

b. **If there was a change, did it relate to a change in partners?** (140)

☐ yes          ☐ no

31. **How is communication between you and full-time workers affected by job sharing?** (225)

☐ benefits     ☐ no effect     ☐ makes more difficult

32. **Do you need special time to communicate with your partner?** (180)

☐ yes          ☐ no

**If yes, do you use:**

☐ overlap time     ☐ time out of work     ☐ other: _____

33. Do you have a formal communication system? (230)

☐ work log
☐ tapes
☐ meet regularly to talk

☐ none
☐ other: _____

*PLEASE CIRCLE ON THE FOLLOWING SCALE THE DEGREE TO WHICH YOU AGREE WITH THESE STATEMENTS (WHEREVER APPLICABLE TO YOUR JOB):*

| | strongly disagree | somewhat disagree | neither agree nor disagree | somewhat agree | strongly agree |
|---|---|---|---|---|---|
| 34. It was difficult to work out the division of responsibilities between you and your partner. (227) | 1 | 2 | 3 | 4 | 5 |
| 35. Training in the mechanics of job sharing would have been helpful in the initial redesign of the position. (222) | 1 | 2 | 3 | 4 | 5 |
| 36. There is a need for close communication between you and your partner. (230) | 1 | 2 | 3 | 4 | 5 |
| 37. Sharing enhances your sense of responsibility to each other. (232) | 1 | 2 | 3 | 4 | 5 |

| | strongly disagree | somewhat disagree | neither agree nor disagree | somewhat agree | strongly agree |
|---|---|---|---|---|---|
| 38. Sharing enhances your sense of commitment to the organization. (231) | 1 | 2 | 3 | 4 | 5 |
| 39. Your effectiveness in work is dependent on your partner's performance. (233) | 1 | 2 | 3 | 4 | 5 |
| 40. Successful sharing depends on compatible personalities. (233) | 1 | 2 | 3 | 4 | 5 |
| 41. Closer collaboration between you and your partner would make job more effective. (226) | 1 | 2 | 3 | 4 | 5 |
| 42. Working fewer hours results in higher energy on the job. (229) | 1 | 2 | 3 | 4 | 5 |
| 43. Collaboration enhances the quality of your work, i.e., "two heads are better than one." (232) | 1 | 2 | 3 | 4 | 5 |
| 44. Sharing your job gives you a greater sense of participation in organizational decision-making. (228) | 1 | 2 | 3 | 4 | 5 |

45. You have a better opportunity to learn on the job because the work is shared (rather than part-time only). (225)  1  2  3  4  5

46. Your job allows flexibility in terms of:

    time  (229)  1  2  3  4  5

    task  (217)  1  2  3  4  5

    place  (204)  1  2  3  4  5

47. You have as good a chance of being promoted as:

a. a non-sharer (part-time)  (184)  1  2  3  4  5

b. as a full-time person in similar position  (192)  1  2  3  4  5

48. Your job-sharing situation represents a clear model of success.  (225)  1  2  3  4  5

49. Indicate which of your partner's personal characteristics have contributed positively to the sharing of your job: *(Please number all relevant items in order of importance to you.)*  (420 mentions)

___ maturity

___ positive competition

___ intelligence

___ openly communicates about problems

___ joyous personality

___ sense of humor

___ brings flowers to the office

___ other: _____

**50. Indicate which of your partner's characteristics have contributed negatively to the sharing of your job:**
*(Please number all relevant items in order of importance to you.)* (152 mentions)

___ defensive about talking
___ overly competitive
___ irresponsible
___ irritating personal habits
___ spends too much time on the job
___ unable to criticize constructively
___ other: _____

**51. You and your partner share responsibilities outside of work:**

a. ☐ housework  (188)
   ☐ family care
   ☐ child care
   ☐ babysitting arrangements
   ☐ other:
   ☐ none

b. ☐ you and your partner share social activities  (105)

**52. What activities fill your non-work time?** *(Please number all relevant items in order of importance to you.)*

a. ___ community and political (volunteering)
   ___ education, studies
   ___ home care      (462 mentions)
   ___ family care
   ___ recreation (sports, hobbies, social)
   ___ other job
   ___ other: _____

b. **If other job, list primary reason:**  (44)

☐ need for additional income
☐ need for full-time work activity
☐ have non-monetary interest in other job
☐ other: _____

185

**53. Do you expect to stay in your current job as a sharer:** (220)

☐ less than 1 year   ☐ 1 - 2 years   ☐ 3 - 5 years   ☐ indefinitely

**54. If planning to leave (or have left) in less than a year, what are (or were) your reasons?** *(Please number all relevant reasons in order of importance to you.)* (101 mentions)

___ position is temporary          ___ job requires too much time
___ financial reasons              ___ had to work more than part-time hours
___ retirement                     ___ difficulties with partner
___ family responsibilities        ___ difficulties with supervisors
___ career change                  ___ other: _____

**55. If you have left this job, was it because you preferred full time?** (238)

☐ yes            ☐ no            ☐ not applicable

## PART IV - PERSONAL DATA AND WORK EXPECTATIONS

**56. Your age range is:** (237)

☐ below 20   ☐ 31 - 40   ☐ 51 - 64
☐ 21 - 30    ☐ 41 - 50   ☐ over 65

**57. Your ethnic background is:** (237)

☐ Caucasian   ☐ Oriental          ☐ other: _____
☐ Black       ☐ Latin-American

**58. Your marital status is:** (234)

☐ single ☐ divorced ☐ widow(er)
☐ married ☐ separated

**59. How many children do you have living with you?** (236)

☐ none ☐ 1 - 2 ☐ 3 - 4 ☐ 5 or more

**60. The age of the youngest child living with you:** (202)

☐ less than 2 ☐ 6 - 11 ☐ 16 - 18 ☐ 23 and older
☐ 2 - 5 ☐ 12 - 15 ☐ 19 - 22 ☐ not applicable

**61. For how many dependents (besides yourself) are you the sole support?** (222)

☐ 1 ☐ 3 ☐ 5 or more
☐ 2 ☐ 4 ☐ none

**62. Your highest academic degree earned was:** (238)

☐ High school ☐ B.A., B.S.W. ☐ Ph.D., M.D.
diploma
☐ A.A. ☐ M.A. ☐ other: _____

**63. This salary is your sole source of income**

    a. for you: (223)    ☐ yes    ☐ no

    b. for your family: (205)    ☐ yes    ☐ no

    c. If not sole source of income, specify other sources: (192) _____

**64. What do you like best, like least about your job?**

**65. What do you think will be the major obstacles to extending job sharing/splitting: organization constraints (i.e., resistance to change, costs, etc.), union contracts, lack of awareness of option, matching of partners, etc.?**

**66. In summation, we would appreciate your comments on any of the following:**

    a. What factors make the shared position successful? (organizational and personal)

    b. What factors make the shared position unsuccessful? (organizational and personal)

    c. How might the organization facilitate shared positions?

    d. How are shared positions qualitatively different from non-shared jobs?